麦格希 中英双语阅读文库

百科百问

第 1 辑

【美】布鲁卡 (Milada Broukal) ●主编

胡亚红 ●译

麦格希中英双语阅读文库编委会 ●编

全国百佳图书出版单位
吉林出版集团股份有限公司

图书在版编目（CIP）数据

百科百问. 第1辑 /（美）布鲁卡 (Milada Broukal)
主编；麦格希中英双语阅读文库编委会编；胡亚红
译. -- 2版. -- 长春：吉林出版集团股份有限公司，
2018.3（2022.1重印）
（麦格希中英双语阅读文库）
ISBN 978-7-5581-4733-3

Ⅰ.①百… Ⅱ.①布… ②麦… ③胡… Ⅲ.①英语—
汉语—对照读物②科学知识—青少年读物 Ⅳ.
①H319.4：Z

中国版本图书馆CIP数据核字(2018)第045917号

百科百问　第1辑

编：麦格希中英双语阅读文库编委会
插　画：齐　航　李延霞
责任编辑：欧阳鹏
封面设计：冯冯翼
开　本：660mm×960mm　1/16
字　数：231千字
印　张：10.25
版　次：2018年3月第2版
印　次：2022年1月第2次印刷

出　版：吉林出版集团股份有限公司
发　行：吉林出版集团外语教育有限公司
地　址：长春市福祉大路5788号龙腾国际大厦B座7层
　　　　邮编：130011
电　话：总编办：0431-81629929
　　　　发行部：0431-81629927　0431-81629921(Fax)
印　刷：北京一鑫印务有限责任公司

ISBN 978-7-5581-4733-3　　　定价：38.00元

▌前 言 *PREFACE*

英国思想家培根说过：阅读使人深刻。阅读的真正目的是获取信息，开拓视野和陶冶情操。从语言学习的角度来说，学习语言若没有大量阅读就如隔靴搔痒，因为阅读中的语言是最丰富、最灵活、最具表现力、最符合生活情景的，同时读物中的情节、故事引人入胜，进而能充分调动读者的阅读兴趣，培养读者的文学修养，至此，语言的学习水到渠成。

"麦格希中英双语阅读文库"在世界范围内选材，涉及科普、社会文化、文学名著、传奇故事、成长励志等多个系列，充分满足英语学习者课外阅读之所需，在阅读中学习英语、提高能力。

◎难度适中

本套图书充分照顾读者的英语学习阶段和水平，从读者的阅读兴趣出发，以难易适中的英语语言为立足点，选材精心、编排合理。

◎精品荟萃

本套图书注重经典阅读与实用阅读并举。既包含国内外脍炙人口、耳熟能详的美文，又包含科普、人文、故事、励志类等多学科的精彩文章。

◎功能实用

本套图书充分体现了双语阅读的功能和优势，充分考虑到读者课外阅读的方便，超出核心词表的词汇均出现在使其意义明显的语境之中，并标注释义。

鉴于编者水平有限，凡不周之处，谬误之处，皆欢迎批评教正。

我们真心地希望本套图书承载的文化知识和英语阅读的策略对提高读者的英语著作欣赏水平和英语运用能力有所裨益。

丛书编委会

Contents

Why Do People Give Gifts for Weddings?

People give gifts for weddings for different reasons. Usually, people want to help the *bride* and *groom*. Many countries have their own customs. In the United States, both families give gifts to the couple. In other places, the customs are very different.

为何人们在婚礼上馈赠礼物？

人们在婚礼上馈赠礼物是出于不同的原因。通常人们是想帮助新娘和新郎。每个国家有各自的习俗。在美国，双方家庭都会馈赠礼物给新婚夫妇。地方不同，习俗也就不一样。

bride *n.* 新娘

groom *n.* 新郎

In India, the groom's family asks for a large payment from the bride's family. The payment is called a *dowry*. Sometimes the payment is a special gift with a *brand* name. For example, some families ask for a Singer sewing machine or a Sony television set. Sometimes the payment is money. The money may be equal to the family's *salary* for two or three years. Both families agree about the money. They agree on how much money the bride's family can *afford* to pay. Some Indian families do not like to have many daughters. It is too expensive! Today in India, a woman with a large salary is the same as a woman with a large dowry.

In the Middle East, the bride's family asks for a large amount of money from the groom. The gift is called a mahr. The mahr is money and sometimes land or a home. In Saudi Arabia, the groom gives a lot of money. He buys clothes for the bride for one year and buys

---

在印度，新郎家庭会要求新娘的家庭支付一大笔钱，即所谓嫁妆。有时可把一件名牌商品作为特别礼物。比如，有的家庭会要求一台"歌唱家"牌的缝纫机或一台索尼电视机。有时就馈赠现金，其数目相当于整个家庭两三年的收入。双方会根据新娘家庭经济承受力的大小商定彩礼数目的多少。所以有些印度家庭不希望有太多女儿，因为那样太昂贵。现在，印度妇女挣得多就表明她嫁妆也多。

而在中东是由新娘家庭向新郎家庭索要大笔钱，这个礼物被称为"mahr"，它有时是钱，也可以是土地或者房屋。在沙特阿拉伯，新郎会给新娘一大笔钱，还会在一年内负责新娘的着装和给新房添置家具。较富

---

dowry *n.* 嫁妆

salary *n.* 工资；薪水

brand *n.* 商标；牌子

afford *v.* 提供；负担得起

furniture for their new home. Rich couples get *expensive* gifts from both parents. The parents often give nice furniture or a new car.

At one time in Saudi Arabia, the mahr for a bride was very, very high. Men could not afford to marry Saudi Arabian women. They married women from Lebanon and Egypt. This was bad for Saudi women. Soon, many Saudi women did not have husbands. The government made new rules. They made it hard to marry a foreigner. Another Middle Eastern country, Oman, had problems, too. Soldiers in the army could not afford to get married. The *sultan* of Oman made a law against large mahr payments. This helped couples in Oman to get married.

A wedding is a very special and important time. People give gifts for different reasons, but one thing is the same. Everybody wants to help the bride and groom start a happy life together.

裕的夫妇会从双方父母那得到非常贵重的礼物，父母们通常会给他们添置家具或新车。

曾经有段时间，沙特阿拉伯的新娘索要的钱款非常多，以至于很多人根本娶不起沙特阿拉伯的姑娘，他们只好娶黎巴嫩或埃及的姑娘。这对沙特的姑娘就很不利，不久很多沙特阿拉伯的姑娘嫁不出去了。于是政府颁布了新法令，使人们很难和外国人结婚。在另一个中东国家安曼也存在同样的问题。军队的士兵没有经济能力结婚，于是阿曼的苏丹就颁布法令禁止高额彩礼，这项举措帮助很多安曼人成了家。

婚礼是一段很特别又很重要的时光，虽然朋友们出于不同的原因馈赠礼物，但有一点是相同的：每个人都希望新娘新郎能开心、幸福地生活在一起。

---

furniture *n.* 家具
at one time 曾经；一度

expensive *adj.* 昂贵的
sultan *n.* 苏丹（某些伊斯兰国家统治者的称号）

How Did Disneyland Start?

One day, a man named Walt Disney took his daughters to an amusement park. At the amusement park, they went on the rides, played games, and saw animals. But the park was not exciting. It was also dirty. He *looked around* and said, "I want to take my children to a better place. I want families to have fun together."

Walt Disney *was famous for* his

迪斯尼乐园是如何创建的?

有一天，沃尔特·迪士尼带他女儿去游乐园。他们骑车，玩游戏，还观赏动物。可他觉得游乐园一点都不刺激而且还特别脏，他环顾四周说："我想带我的孩子去更好玩的地方，我希望家人能非常开心地在一起。"

沃尔特·迪士尼因其电影和卡通片闻名于世。现在，他开始策划一

---

look around 环顾；环视　　　　　　　be famous for 因……而闻名

movies. He was also famous for his *cartoons*. Now Disney started to think about a new park. He wanted a park with different parts with special names. One part was "Fantasyland" and another part was "Adventureland" . He also wanted to use ideas from his movies and cartoons. His most popular cartoon was Mickey Mouse. Disney wanted Mickey Mouse and other cartoon people to walk around the park and talk to the *guests*.

Disney's dream of a special park took many years to come true. People did not understand his ideas. Nobody wanted to give him money. So Disney used all his own money to build the park. On July 17, 1955, Disneyland opened in Anaheim, California. It was an *immediate hit*. The first year, about five million people went to Disneyland. People came from all over the United States and all over the world.

Walt Disney wanted Disneyland to be perfect. Every night,

个新的乐园，一个不同位置有各自特别的名字的乐园。这部分叫"童话世界"，另一部分叫"冒险乐园"。他甚至还想把他从电影和卡通片里得到的灵感运用到这上面。他最受欢迎的卡通人物是米老鼠，他希望米老鼠和其他卡通人物能游走于乐园中和游客攀谈。

迪士尼关于创建一个别出心裁的乐园的梦想很多年后才得以实现，因为人们并不能领会他的意图，没人愿意捐资。迪士尼把他毕生积蓄都用来修建乐园。这个乐园于1955年7月17日在加利福尼亚州的阿纳海姆正式成立。刚成立便引起了巨大的轰动，仅第一年，就接待了来自美国和世界各地的近五百万游客。

沃尔特·迪士尼希望迪士尼乐园尽善尽美。每晚，工人们都会清洗

---

cartoon *n.* 卡通片；动画片

immediate *adj.* 立刻的；马上的

guest *n.* 客人；来宾

hit *n.* 轰动一时的人或事物；成功

workers washed the streets. They *made sure* the streets were clean. They also made sure there was no chewing *gum* on the ground. They painted the signs again at night. They wanted the signs to look new.

Disneyland always had many plants and flowers. But Disney did not want any signs that said, "Do not walk on the plants." So every year, the workers changed 800,000 plants and put in new ones.

Disney wanted the workers to be happy and clean all the time. He started a special school for his workers called the University of Disneyland. The workers learned to be happy and polite to guests. They could not wear *perfume*, jewelry, or bright nail polish. They had to follow rules for how to dress and how to wear their hair.

Walt Disney became very rich. He was a *millionaire*. He died in 1966, but his dream of more Disneylands came true. In 1971, Walt Disney World opened in Orlando, Florida. Today, there are Disneylands in Tokyo and Paris.

街道以确保乐园里街道一尘不染，还得确保地面没有口香糖。他们还会刷新各种路标，使路标看起来像新的一样。

迪士尼乐园里还有许多植物和花草，但迪士尼并不希望乐园里有"不准践踏植物"的标志，因此每年都会将八十万株植物更换成新的。

迪士尼希望自己的员工既能愉快的工作又能保持整洁的面貌，他为员工开办了一所很特别的大学——迪士尼乐园大学。学校教育员工要愉快、礼貌地迎接客人；不能喷香水，佩戴首饰或涂指甲油。他们还学习一些如何着装，留何种发型的礼节。

沃尔特·迪士尼富裕起来，变成了百万富翁。他死于1966年，但他希望开办更多迪士尼乐园的梦想变成了现实。1971年，迪士尼乐园在奥兰多、佛罗里达相继开放。迄今，东京、巴黎也都有迪士尼乐园。

---

make sure 确信；确保   gum *n.* 口香糖
perfume *n.* 香水   millionaire *n.* 百万富翁

3

Who Is Andrew Carnegie?

Andrew Carnegie was born in 1835 in Scotland. He was from a poor family. When he was twelve, his family moved to the United States. They wanted a better life.

The Carnegie family lived in Pittsburgh, Pennsylvania. Andrew started to work *right away*. He got a job in a factory. He was a good worker, but he didn't like the job.

安德鲁·卡内基是谁?

1835年,安德鲁·卡内基出生在苏格兰一个贫苦的家庭。他12岁时,举家迁往美国寻求更幸福的生活。

安德鲁家住在宾夕法尼亚州的匹兹堡。他很快在一家工厂找了份工作并且成了一名好工人,但他并不喜欢这份工作。后来,他去了宾夕法尼亚

right away 立刻

Later, he changed his job. He worked at the Pennsylvania Railroad Company. Everybody there liked Andrew. He did many different jobs. His salary got higher every year.

In his free time, Andrew loved to read. He lived near Colonel James Anderson. Colonel Anderson was a rich man with many books. He let young boys use his library for free. In those days, the United States did not have free public libraries. Andrew read *as much as possible*. He read *throughout* his life. He always thought that reading was very important.

Andrew learned a lot at the railroad company. He *realized* that the railroad was very important for big countries. He had an idea to start a business with railroads. He saved all his money and opened a business. He was thirty years old.

First, his company made bridges for the railroads. Ten years later, they made steel. The Carnegie Steel Company became the

---

铁路公司，在那里他受到了大家的欢迎。他做各种不同的工作，薪水一年比一年高。

业余时间，他喜欢看书。他跟詹姆士·安迪生上校是邻居。詹姆士·安迪生上校家很有钱，家里有丰富的藏书。他允许安德鲁无偿使用他家图书馆，而当时美国没有免费的公共图书馆。安德鲁都尽可能多的阅读，他整个一生都在阅读，他一直认为读书对人类来说是非常重要的。

安德鲁在铁路公司学到了很多东西，他意识到铁路对一个大国来说至关重要。他开始计划创办与铁路有关的公司。他拿出所有积蓄创建了公司，当时年仅30岁。

最初，他的公司是为铁路修建桥梁。十年后，他开始炼钢并且使卡内基钢铁公司成了美国最大的一家钢铁公司。为桥梁，机器和其他很多项

---

as much as possible 尽可能多

realize *v.* 认识到；意识到

throughout *prep.* 遍及；贯穿

largest company in the United States. They made steel for bridges, machines, and many other things. People called Carnegie the "Steel King". Soon he was the richest man in the world.

Carnegie liked to make money. But he believed it was very important to help other people. In 1901, he sold his company for $480 million. He started to *give away* his money to make new libraries and colleges all over the United States. He built 2,811 libraries. Carnegie also gave a lot of money to people who worked for *peace*. In 1903, he gave $1.5 million to build a Peace Palace in the Netherlands.

Andrew Carnegie died in 1919. He was eighty-four years old. During his life, he gave away nearly all of his money. He gave away over $350 million for education and peace. There are colleges, libraries, hospitals, and parks named after Andrew Carnegie. He has helped millions of people all over the world to study and learn.

目提供钢铁。由此，他被称作"钢铁大王"，不久，他就成了世界上最富有的人。

卡内基喜欢挣钱，但他同时也意识到帮助别人的重要性。1901年，他以四亿八千万的价格售出了他的公司。卡内基用这些钱在美国兴建了许多图书馆和大学，其中图书馆就有2811所。卡内基还捐助那些为和平而努力的人们。1903年，他出资一百五十万美元在荷兰修建了和平宫殿。

安德鲁·卡内基于1919年去世，终年84岁。他一生的积蓄几乎全用于了慈善事业，他为教育与和平事业捐助了近三亿五百万美元。有许多大学，图书馆，医院和公园都是以他的名字命名的，他为世界上数百万人的学习提供了帮助。

---

give away 赠送；捐赠　　　　　　　　　　　peace *n.* 和平

What Is Life Like in Antarctica?

Antarctica is like no other place in the world. It is *unique*. It is very big. It is like the United States and Australia together. Antarctica is the coldest place in the world. The *temperature* is sometimes -125°F (-87℃). August and September are the coldest months because there is no sun.

Antarctica is at the southern tip of the world. It is the highest

南极洲的生活是什么样的?

南极洲与世界其他任何地方都不同，它独一无二，辽阔宽广。其面积相当于美国和澳大利亚领土的总和。南极洲是世界上最冷的地方，有时最低温度达到零下87度。由于南极洲八、九月份没有太阳照射，因而这两个月是那儿最冷的时候。

南极洲在地球的最南端，是大陆的最高点，近一万英尺高。南极洲上

---

unique *adj.* 唯一的；独一无二的　　temperature *n.* 温度；体温

continent. It is 10,000 feet high. Antarctica also has very strong winds. The wind sometimes blows two hundred miles an hour. It is also the driest place in the world. Antarctica is drier than the Sahara Desert!

Antarctica is also empty. There are huge *glacier* and ice everywhere. A glacier is an area of ice that moves slowly. The ice and glaciers are beautiful. But most plants and land animals cannot live on the ice. It is too cold. There are no trees, no rivers, and no cities in Antarctica. There are no land animals. Only penguins and other sea birds live there.

Antarctica does not *belong to* any one country. In fact, every country owns Antarctica. More than twenty countries have stations in Antarctica. A station is a place where scientists do experiments. There are *separate* stations for different countries. The scientists are the only people who live in Antarctica. In all, over four thousand people live at the stations in the summer. Over one thousand people

---

空有强风，有时风速达到每小时二百英里。它还是世界上最干的地方，比撒哈拉沙漠都干燥。

南极洲很空旷，到处都是大片的冰山和雪块。冰山会慢慢地移动。雪块和冰山非常美丽。由于冰太冷，大多数植物和陆地动物都不能在冰上生活。南极洲太冷了，那里没有树，没有河流，也没有城市和陆地动物，只有企鹅和海鸟生活在那里。

南极洲不属于任何国家，事实上，每个国家在南极洲都有发言权。有近二十个国家在南极洲设有考察站。在那里科学家进行实验，不同的国家设有不同的考察站。南极洲只有科学家居住。在夏季，共四千多人居住在

---

glacier *n.* 冰河；冰川   belong to 属于
separate *adj.* 不同的；单独的

live there in the winter.

Life on an Antarctica station is hard. It is like life on a space station. The sun shines for six months, and then it is night for six months. People usually have problems with sleeping and eating. They eat more because they are not busy. In an emergency, it is hard to get help. In 1999, an American doctor named Jerri Nielsen realized she was sick. She had cancer. It was winter, and airplanes could not land in Antarctica. She was the only doctor there. Dr. Nielsen had no choice. She had to stay. An airplane *dropped* medicine to her, and she *took care of* herself. Several months later, Dr. Nielsen returned to the United States to get special medical help.

Today, more and more people visit Antarctica. Ships go to Antarctica during the summer months from November to February. People want to visit this unusual place, but they don't want to live there!

考察站。就是冬季也有一千多人居住在那儿。

考察站的生活非常艰苦，就像在太空站一样。连续六个月的太阳照射后是六个月的黑夜。这里，人们睡觉和吃饭都成问题，由于他们不忙，吃的也比平常多。当有紧急情况时，一般都得不到救助。1999年，一位名叫洁莉·尼尔森的美国医生患上了癌症，而此时正值冬天，飞机无法到达南极洲，在那儿，只有她是医生。她没有其他选择只好留在那里开展自我治疗，通过飞机给她送来了药品。几个月后，她回到了美国接受专门的治疗。

现在，有越来越多的人去南极洲观光，每年的十一月到第二年二月是南极洲的夏季，这时有游客来到这里，但人们只是想参观这个特殊的地方，没有人想在这里生活。

---

drop *v.* 使（某物）落下   take care of 照顾

Where Do People Live Under the Ground?

One place where people live under the ground is a small town called Coober Pedy. Coober Pedy is in the *Outback* of south Australia. Most of the people in Coober Pedy are miners. Miners dig under the ground. They *look for* gold or special stones. Coober Pedy is famous for *opals*.

Opals are beautiful white stones. People put opals in jewelry.

Miners *discovered* opals in Coober Pedy in 1915. At that time,

---

哪里的人们居住在地下?

库柏派蒂的小镇位于澳大利亚南部内陆地区。那里的人们居住在地下，他们中大多数是矿工，在地下挖煤和寻找金矿以及一些特别的矿石。库柏派蒂盛产蛋白石，那是种很漂亮的白色石头，人们把它嵌入珠宝中。

那里的矿工们是在1915年发现蛋白石的，那时，许多矿工住在地下

---

outback *n.* 内地　　　　　　look for 寻找
opal *n.* 蛋白石　　　　　　discover *v.* 发现；发觉

many miners lived in simple holes under the ground. *Aboriginal* people laughed at them. The Aboriginal people are the *native* people of Australia. They called the area kupa piti. This means "white man in a hole" in their language.

Today, the homes are not simple holes. About four thousand people live in Coober Pedy. About half the people live under the ground. Coober Pedy has homes, restaurants, hotels, and churches. It is like other towns. But the people don't have a *view*. A new underground house with five rooms costs about $25,000. Some homes have swimming pools!

The people of Coober Pedy live underground for different reasons. One reason is there are no trees. The last tree died in 1971. People need wood from trees to build houses. The main *reason* why people live underground is the very hot weather. The temperature in the summer goes up to 122℉[50℃]. Underground, the temperature

---

很简陋的洞里，遭到了澳大利亚当地土著人的嘲笑，他们把矿工居住的地方叫"kupa piti"，在他们语言里是"洞里的白人"的意思。

现在他们的房屋不再是简陋的地洞了。现在大约有四千人居住在库柏派蒂，其中有一半的人住在地下。这个小镇像其他小镇一样，那里有房屋，餐馆，旅店和教堂。但由于这里的人们住在地下，在家里无法观赏到户外的风景。一座新的五居室的地下房屋售价大约是二万五千美元。有的家庭甚至还有游泳池。

库柏派蒂的人们住在地下的原因有很多。其中一个原因是小镇里没有树，那里的树在1971年时就灭绝了，而人们需要树木来建房屋。人们住在地下最主要的原因是天气过于炎热。夏天，这里的温度会达到50度，而此时地下的温度只有25度。

---

aboriginal *adj.* 土著的；原始的
view *n.* 景色；风景

native *adj.* 本国的；本地的
reason *n.* 原因

is 77°F [25°C].

People also live under the ground in the Sahara Desert in south Tunisia. It is very hot and there are no trees. The people there are called Berbers. The Berbers dig deep holes in the ground. Many houses have two or three floors, but they are simple. Air and light come through an open hole. There are about seven hundred of these holes.

Thousands of years ago, people hid underground in Cappadocia, Turkey. People still live there today. It is a beautiful place with good weather. *In the future*, more people will live under the ground. They will have different reasons. Japan has a lot of people and little land. Japan wants to build a city under the ground. The name of the city will be Alice City. About 100,000 people will live there. It will have offices, hotels, sports centers, and *theaters*.

Underground cities are very interesting, of course. But can people live with no sun and no sky?

　　在突尼斯南部撒哈拉沙漠的人们也住在地下，那里也没有树，天气也很炎热。人们把那里的人称做巴巴里人，他们住在地下的深洞里。许多房屋虽然有两三层，但是很简陋，空气和阳光可以从通风口进来，这样的通风口大约有七百多个。

　　几千年前，土耳其卡帕多奇亚地区的人们隐居在地下，至今，他们仍住在地下。那地方不仅风光宜人天气也好，将来会有更多的人出于不同的原因在那里定居。由于日本人多地少，他们想建一座地下城市并起名叫爱丽斯城。那里将会有十万人居住，不仅有办公室，旅店，体育中心，还有剧院。

　　地下城市当然很有趣，但人们愿意生活在没有蓝天和太阳的地方吗？

---

in the future 将来 　　　　　　　　　　　　theater *n.* 剧院

Why Do People Decorate Their Bodies?

People decorate their bodies for many reasons. They also decorate in different ways. Some groups of people have decorated their bodies for thousands of years. Other people want to look *attractive*. Other people want to belong to a group.

Some people decorate their lips, ears, and neck to be beautiful. For example, in Africa, the Surmese women wear a *plate* in

为何人们要装扮自己呢？

人们装扮自己是出于很多原因的，他们用不同的方式装扮自己。有些地方的人们装扮自己已经有几千年的历史了。有的是希望自己看起来很迷人，有些则是想有一种归属感。

有的人把嘴唇，耳朵和脖子装饰得很漂亮。例如，非洲的萨米斯妇女在下嘴唇佩带金属片。她们是如何做到的呢？首先，母亲在女儿的下嘴唇

attractive *adj.* 吸引人的；有魅力的   plate *n.* 金属牌

their bottom lip. How do they do this? First, a mother makes a hole in her daughter's bottom lip. Then she *stretches* the lip. Then she puts a small plate in it. As the daughter gets older, she puts in bigger and bigger plates. Other people in Africa put plates in their ears. They want the bottom of their ears to hang to their shoulders.

The Pa Daung women in Myanmar are called "giraffe women." They have very long necks, like giraffes. The women wear metal rings to stretch their necks. They wear more rings as they get older. Their necks become longer. Their necks are sometimes two or three times the *normal* size. Some women die if they take off the rings.

People also *decorate* their teeth to be beautiful. Many Americans and Europeans like white, straight teeth. They spend a lot of money to fix and clean their teeth. This is not true in other parts of the world. In east Africa, some people pull out their bottom teeth. They

上打个洞，然后把嘴唇扩张，这时放一块小的金属片在里面。随着女儿年龄的增长，放入的金属片就会逐渐增大。非洲的其他地区的人们把金属片放在耳朵上，他们希望耳垂能垂到肩膀上。

缅甸的帕达妇女被称作"长颈鹿妇女"，因为她们的脖子很长，像长颈鹿。妇女们用金属环使她们的脖子伸长。年纪越大戴的金属环就越多，脖子就越长。有时，她们的脖子比正常长两三倍，但她们如果把环摘下来，有些人就会死掉。

人们有时也把牙齿装饰得很好看。许多美国人和欧洲人都喜欢洁白、整齐的牙齿。他们会在坚固和清洁牙齿上花费很多钱。而在世界上的其他地区，情况就不一样了。在东非，有的人把下牙全部拔掉使得上牙能突出

stretch *v.* 伸展；伸长　　　　　　　　　　　　normal *adj.* 正常的
decorate *v.* 装饰

want their top teeth to *stick out*. In some parts of Asia, women used to paint their teeth black to look beautiful. Today, young people do not do this. In Indonesia, boys and girls *file* their teeth. A person with filed teeth will have a good and healthy life.

People around the world always liked tattoos. Europeans learned about tattoos around 1770. A famous English explorer named Captain Cook went to Tahiti. He saw people there with tattoos. The Tahitians called the decoration tatou. From this, we get the word tattoo. The Tahitians taught Cook and his sailors how to make tattoos. The sailors returned to England, and other people liked their tattoos. Soon tattoos *spread* to the rest of Europe. Many sailors still have tattoos.

Today, many different types of people have tattoos. For some people, body decorations are attractive. For other people, they are strange.

来。在亚洲某些地区，妇女们会把牙齿涂成黑色，使自己看起来漂亮些。而现在的年轻人不会这么做。在印尼，男孩女孩们会把牙锉光滑，他们认为这样做就会拥有美好而健康的生活。

世界各地的人们都喜欢文身。欧洲人在大约公元1770年就学会了文身。一位英国著名的探险家库克船长去海地时就看到那里的人们有文身。海地语把这叫"tatou"，由此才有后来的"tattoo（文身）"。海地人教会了库克船长和他的海员们如何文身。这些船员回到英国后，其他人也很喜欢他们的文身，于是文身就在欧洲其他地方传播开来。现在许多海员仍然保留着文身。

现在，各种类型的人都有文身。对有的人来说，文身看起来很迷人，对另一些人来说，文身看起来则有些奇怪。

---

stick out 伸出   file *v.* 锉

spread *v.* 传播；散布

7

How Did the Red Cross Start?

In 1859, a Swiss man named Henry Dunant went to Italy. He went there on business. There was a war in the town of Solferino. Dunant saw the war, and he was *shocked*. There were thousands of wounded men. Nobody was there to take care of them.

Dunant asked the people in the town to help the wounded men. Later, he

红十字会是如何创立的？

1859年，一位叫亨利·杜南的瑞士人去意大利出差，他看到那里的索弗利诺小镇战火连连，亲眼看见了几千名军人受伤却无人照顾，对这一惨状感到很震惊。

于是，杜南召集镇上的人帮助这些伤者。后来，他写了本书《索弗利诺镇的记忆》，他想了个很好的办法帮助战争中的人们。他希望每个国家

---

shocked *adj.* 震惊的

wrote a book called *A Memory of Solferino*. He had a good idea to help people in wars. He wanted every country to have volunteers. The *volunteers* take care of the *wounded* people in wars.

In 1863, Dunant and four other Swiss men started the Red Cross. A year later, twelve countries signed a paper in Geneva, Switzerland. Dunant traveled to other countries. He wanted to make the Red Cross bigger and better all over the world.

By now, Dunant was famous. But his own business had problems. His business had no money. Some people in Geneva were angry because they lost money, too. Dunant *resigned* from the Red Cross. Now he had no money and no home. He slept in the streets and had nothing to eat. For twenty years, he lived on different streets in Switzerland. In 1890, a teacher found him in a Swiss village. The teacher told everybody that Dunant was alive. But nobody cared.

都能有志愿者帮助那些战争中受伤的人们。

1863年，杜南和另外四个瑞士人成立了红十字会。一年后，十二个国家在瑞士日内瓦签署协议。他开始游走于各个国家想让红十字会规模更大，功效更好。

后来，杜南成了名人，但他的事业出现了危机，已经没有一点运作资金了。在日内瓦也有人因生意赔钱非常气愤。杜南辞去了红十字会的职务，他身无分文，无家可归，每天都睡在大街上，三餐无着落。二十年间，他每天在瑞士的不同街道上过夜。1890年的一天，有位老师在瑞士的一个乡村发现了他，当他把杜南还活着的消息告诉人们时，已无人对此感兴趣了。

---

volunteer *n.* 志愿者   wounded *adj.* 受伤的
resign *v.* 辞职

Dunant became very sick. He went to a hospital for the poor in the town of Heiden. Dunant stayed in the same room for eighteen years. It was Room 12. In 1895, a *journalist* found him and wrote about him. Then Dunant became famous again. People gave him prizes and money. But Dunant stayed in Room 12.

Dunant died in 1910. There was no funeral ceremony. He wanted everything to be simple. Dunant gave his money to the hospital workers. He also gave money for a "free bed" in the hospital. This "free bed" was for the poor sick people of Heiden.

The *symbol* of the Red Cross is a red cross on a white flag. It is the *reverse* of the flag of Switzerland. Muslim countries have a red *crescent*. A crescent looks like a half-moon. Today, more than 170 countries are part of the Red Cross and Red Crescent. The volunteers help people in many ways. Everybody remembers Henry Dunant and his good idea.

　　杜南生病后去了海登镇上的一家专为穷人看病的医院。在十二号病房里待了十八年。1895年，有位记者发现他后写了篇关于他的报道，他又成了名人。人们嘉奖他并给他很多钱，但他仍留在十二号病房。

　　杜南死于1910年，死后没举行葬礼，他希望一切从简。他把所有的钱都捐给了医院的工作人员，还支付了他使用床位的费用。这个床位是海登镇专门为贫苦的病人准备的。

　　红十字会的标志是一面白旗上有个红色十字，是瑞士国旗的反面。伊斯兰国家有红新月会，新月就像半月形。现在大约有一百七十个国家是红十字会和红新月会的成员国。人们从志愿者那里得到了多方面的帮助。每个人都会记得亨利·杜南和他的好主意。

---

journalist *n.* 新闻记者
reverse *n.* 相反；反面

symbol *n.* 符号，象征
crescent *n.* 新月形；月牙形

Who Are the Blue Men of the Sahara?

The Blue Men of the Sahara is a name for the Tuareg people. People call them this name because they wear blue clothes. There are between 300,000 and one million Tuareg today. They have lived in the Sahara Desert for thousands of years. It is hot, dry, and windy there. Their lives are difficult because of the *desert* weather and life.

谁是撒哈拉的蓝人?

人们把图阿列格人称为撒哈拉的蓝人，因为他们都穿蓝色的衣服。目前世界上图阿列格人数量大约在三十万到一百万之间。他们已在撒哈拉沙漠定居几千年了。那里天气炎热，干燥，而且风还很大，这种沙漠气候和生活方式给他们的生存带来了极大的挑战。

desert *n.* 沙漠

The Tuareg do not live in one place. They move from place to place to find water and food for their animals. The Tuareg live in groups of four or five families. Everybody helps each other. The men take care of the animals. The women put up the tents. The Tuareg live and sleep in the tents. Tuareg tents *are* usually *made of* animal skins, but today some Tuareg have plastic tents.

The Tuareg dress in a special way. The men cover their faces. The women do not. The men travel a lot in the desert. They need to protect their faces from the dry air and sand.

The Tuareg men have many customs about their face. They start to cover their faces at age twenty-five. They do not cover their faces for friends. They use black or white cloth. The cloth is five yards long. They *wrap* the cloth around their face and neck. You see their eyes, but you don't see their nose and mouth.

图阿列格人并不只在同一个地方定居，为了给牲畜寻找水和食物会四处迁徙。图阿列格人一般都是四五个家庭住在一起，大家互相帮助。男人们照顾牲畜，女人们支帐篷。饮食起居都在帐篷里。帐篷通常是由动物皮做成的，但现在有的图阿列格人用塑料帐篷。

图阿列格人的穿着很特别，男人们都会把自己的脸遮住，而女人们则不会，因为男人经常在沙漠中穿行，需要保护自己的脸抵御干燥的空气和风沙。

图阿列格人有许多关于脸的习俗，男子一般在25岁时开始遮脸，但在朋友面前并不这样做。他们一般使用五码长的白色或黑色的布将脸和脖子裹起来。能看见他们的眼睛，但你看不见鼻子和嘴巴。

---

be made of　由······制成　　　　　　　　　　wrap　v.　用······包裹

Every Tuareg man wraps his cloth in a unique way. In this way, everyone knows each other. On special *occasions*, they cover their faces with blue cloth. The blue cloth *rubs* on their faces. Then their faces are blue. The blue cloth is very expensive, so the rich Tuareg have blue faces. Rich women wear a blue shawl around their shoulders and arms. They rub the *shawl* on their faces. They want blue faces, too!

Tuareg men marry women from the same group. They often marry cousins. The Tuareg women have a lot of freedom. They decide important things about their lives. The Tuareg women have long hair and are very beautiful.

Today, many Tuareg do not live in the desert. Countries around the Sahara Desert do not want groups of people going from place to place. Many Tuareg now live in towns. Soon it will be hard to find the Blue Men of the Sahara.

每个图阿列格人都用不同的方式裹脸，因此相互之间都能识别出来。在特殊的场合他们会用蓝布裹脸。蓝布擦在脸上使整个脸都变成了蓝色。蓝布非常昂贵，因此只有有钱的图阿列格人才会是蓝脸。有钱的妇女披蓝色的披肩，她们用披肩擦自己的脸好让自己也变成蓝脸。

图阿列格人都娶自己同族的姑娘，通常与表亲结婚。图阿列格妇女非常自由，生活中的许多大事都由她们做主，图阿列格妇女头发很长，长得也很漂亮。

现在，许多图阿列格人都不住在沙漠，撒哈拉沙漠周围的国家不希望群居的人们到处迁徙。许多图阿列格人都居住在镇上。不久，撒哈拉沙漠的蓝人将成为一道稀有的风景线。

---

occasion *n.* 场合   rub *v.* 擦；摩擦
shawl *n.* 披巾；披肩

What Is Canada's Favorite Sport?

C anada's favorite sport is ice hockey. All over Canada today, men, women, boys, and girls play hockey. Hockey began in Canada. But we do not know exactly how it began.

At first, hockey did not have rules. Then, in 1880, Canadian students at McGill University in Montreal made the

加拿大最受欢迎的体育运动是什么？

在加拿大最受欢迎的体育运动是冰球。现在在加拿大，男女老少都喜欢玩冰球。冰球起源加拿大，但我们无法确切地知道它是如何发起的。

起初，冰球的玩法没什么规则。到了1880年，加拿大蒙特利尔的麦吉尔大学的学生为冰球运动制定了一些基本规则。在1911年和1912年间

at first 起初；最先

first rules for ice hockey. These rules changed in 1911 and 1912. The new rules had lines on the ice to make special *areas*. There were also six players on a team. This is *similar* to hockey today.

Ice hockey is the world's fastest game. Players often skate thirty miles an hour. They get tired quickly. Often, hockey players leave a game and other players come in. In hockey, players use a stick to hit a puck. A puck is like a ball, but it is flat. It *slides* on the ice. It is better to use a cold puck because it slides faster. Players put the puck in the freezer before a game. In some games, players use more than thirty pucks!

Hockey looks easy to play, but it isn't easy. Players try to hit the puck into the other team's *goal*. The puck goes faster than the players. Pucks go about one hundred miles an hour. Hockey is a

---

人们修改了这些规则，在冰上用线划出特定的区域，每队有六名选手。这跟今天的冰球运动规则很相似。

冰球是世界上最快的体育项目，参赛者在冰上每小时滑行三十米，很容易就累了，冰球运动员一般都是替换的。冰球运动员用木棍使冰球滚动，冰球就像普通的球一样，只不过是扁平的。它在冰上滑动。由于凉的冰球滚动速度较快，人们一般都喜欢用凉冰球。在一场比赛前，人们都会把冰球放入冰箱里冷冻，有时一场比赛会使用三十多个冰球。

冰球玩起来好像很容易，但事实上并非如此。参赛者需将冰球打入对方的球门。冰球以每小时上百英里的速度滚动，比球员的速度还快。冰球

---

area *n.* 地区；区域

slide *v.* （使）滑动；（使）滑行

similar *adj.* 相似的；类似的

goal *n.* 球门

dangerous game. Many players get hurt. Today, players wear special clothes to protect their bodies. The player near the goal wears a *mask* to protect his face. A player with no mask can break his nose or teeth. In the past, there were many players with no front teeth.

Professional hockey teams in Canada and the United States play in the NHL. This means the National Hockey League. The NHL started in 1917. Today the NHL has thirty teams in North America. Twenty-four of the teams are in the United States, but most of the players are Canadian. In the spring, millions of people watch the final hockey game of the year on television. The winner gets the Stanley Cup. The Stanley Cup is the *prize* for the best hockey team.

People around the world play hockey now. It is popular in the Olympics. But hockey will always be Canada's special game.

是种很危险的运动，许多球员都会受伤。现在，人们玩冰球时都会穿上特殊的衣服保护自己，守门员也会戴上面罩保护自己的脸。如果他们不戴面罩，鼻子或牙齿就可能会受伤。过去，许多球员就因此没有了门牙。

加拿大和美国的职业冰球队都在国家冰球联盟里打球。国家冰球联盟创建于1917年，现在在北美有30支球队。其中有24支在美国，但大多数队员都是加拿大人。春季，有几百万人通过电视观看冰球决赛。最后胜出的球队会获得斯坦利杯，这是冰球运动员的最高荣誉。

现在世界各地的人们都玩冰球，这项运动在奥林匹克运动中也深受欢迎，但冰球将会一直是加拿大的特别体育运动。

---

dangerous *adj.* 危险的
professional *adj.* 专业的；职业的

mask *n.* 面具；口罩
prize *n.* 奖品；奖金

Where Is the Outback?

About one-half of Australia is desert. This area is the Outback. The name comes from the words "out in the back of the mountains and cities". The weather is very hot and *dry*, and the winds are *strong*. Sometimes there is no rain for many years. But when

---

澳洲内陆在哪里？

澳大利亚一半的领土是沙漠，这块领土被称为澳洲内陆。这个名字原意是"山脉和城市背后的外面"。这里的天气炎热干燥，风很大，有时多年都不会降雨。但一旦下雨，遍地都是水，因此很少有人居住在澳洲内陆。

---

dry *adj.* 干的　　　　　　　　　　strong *adj.* 强壮的；强大的

it rains, there is water everywhere! Not many people live in the Outback.

The people in the Outback have cattle or sheep farms. The farms are called stations. The stations are very big. Some stations are as big as a small country. Life is difficult because everything is far away. Sometimes it takes a day or two to drive to the next station. Towns are usually far away, too. People go to town once a week or once a month.

The station homes are very large because they have many *purposes*. They must be big so visitors can sleep there. Houses also have large rooms to keep extra things. Families buy a lot of food and *supplies* in town.

Life in the Outback is different in other ways. People get mail once a week. Children don't go to school every day. They study with a school called the School of the Air. The teacher and student

---

澳洲内陆的人们都有农场放牧牛或羊，这些农场被称作牧场，牧场都非常大，有的甚至相当于一个小乡村。由于交通不便，那里的生活很艰苦，有时需要行驶一两天才能到达下个牧场。城镇离牧场也很远，人们一般一周去一次或一个月一次。

牧场房屋有很多用途，因此一般都特别大。这样，到访者也能在那里寄宿。房屋一般都有很大的房间用于保存其他物品。一般家庭都在镇上购买大量食品和生活必需品。

澳洲内陆的生活方式与别的地方有很大不同。人们一周才能接一次邮件。孩子们不是每天都去上学，他们的学校叫空气学校。老师和学生都通

---

purpose *n.* 目的；用途   supply *n.* 供应品

talk to each other with a special radio. Most stations have an area for airplanes to land. It is like the station's own airport. Sick people call the Royal Flying Doctor service. A doctor gives advice over the radio. In an emergency, the doctor *picks up* the sick people in an airplane. Then they go to the nearest hospital.

People in the Outback are careful when they travel. Before a farmer travels to town, he tells a friend. The friend knows what time the farmer is coming. If the farmer is late, his friend knows there is a problem. The friend will look for the farmer. People must know how to do many things. They must know how to fix their car if it *breaks down*. They always carry extra gasoline, water, and parts for their car.

Life in the Outback is very difficult, but it is good, too. Here you are close to nature, and there are many unusual animals. You also have a lot of freedom.

过一种特殊收音机交流。许多牧场都留有一块空地供飞机的起升降落，就像是牧场的私人飞机场。病人都把这项服务称作皇家飞行医生。医生都通过收音机给病人指导。在紧急情况下，医生乘飞机来把病人接走送到最近的医院医治。

澳洲内陆的人外出时都很谨慎。村民们去城镇前都会告诉朋友，使他得知自己何时能回来。如果回来晚了，朋友便知道他可能遇到了麻烦，就会去找他。这里的人们必须知道很多生活常识：比如汽车坏了如何修理等。外出时他们一般都会带多余的汽油，水和汽车零件。

虽然澳洲内地的生活很艰苦，但同时也有很多好处。在这里，你能够贴近自然，看见很多不同寻常的动物。同时，你也很自由。

---

pick up　用车接某人　　　　　　　　　　break down　抛锚；发生故障

11

Why Is the Elephant Important in Thailand?

Elephants are a very important part of Thailand's history. They are symbols of *power* and peace. They are strong and *gentle* at the same time. But many years ago, they also did important work. They helped the Thai people get wood from their forests.

In the past, the Thai people *cut down* a

大象在泰国为何如此重要？

象是泰国文化中非常重要的组成部分，是权力和和平的象征。他们既强壮又温柔。许多年前，大象身肩重任，负责帮助泰国人们把木材从森林中运出来。

过去，泰国人砍伐了很多树木。1989年，政府下令禁止砍伐，希望

---

power *n.* 权力；能力
cut down 砍倒

gentle *adj.* 温和的；文雅的

lot of trees. In 1989, the government made a law to stop this. They wanted to keep the trees in the forest. Today, the Thai people cut down only a few trees. Some elephants work in the forests to help them. The forests are in the mountains. Many trucks and machines cannot go up the mountains. But elephants can. Men cut down the trees, and the elephants pick up the trees. Then the elephants carry the trees to the river. The trees *float* down the river to other men. The men cut the trees into pieces of wood.

In the past, elephants *trained* for many years to learn how to work. Each elephant had its own trainer, or *mahout*. A mahout spent his life with the same elephant. Fathers wanted their sons to be mahouts, too. Mahouts bought baby elephants for their sons. First, the baby elephant stayed with its mother. When the elephant was three years old, it lived with the boy. The boy and the elephant grew up together. The boy took care of the elephant. They learned a lot about each

---

能恢复森林的原貌。现在，泰国人很少砍伐树木。一些大象在森林里工作，这些森林都在山区，卡车和机器无法到达那里，但大象能。人们把树砍倒后就由这些大象拾起来搬运到河边。树木顺水而下，人们把这些树劈成木材。

过去，人们会花很多年的时间训练大象如何工作，每头大象都有专门的训练者或象夫。象夫一生陪伴同一头大象。好多父亲也希望自己的儿子成为象夫。象夫为他们的儿子买回幼象。起初，幼象是与母象生活在一起的，当它长到3岁时，就和象夫的儿子住一起，他们一起成长。通过孩子对幼象的照顾，他们间能增进很多了解。

---

float *v.* 漂浮；浮动　　　　　　　　　　　train *v.* 训练
mahout *n.* 象夫；管象人

other.

A mahout trained, fed, and took care of his elephant. This was a difficult job. An elephant eats 550 pounds(250 kilos) of plants and drinks 80 gallons(300 liters) of water every day! It trained every day for six hours in the morning. The elephant *got used to* the mahout. The elephant remembered the mahout's voice and smell. It understood its mahout's *instructions*. The elephant obeyed its mahout. It did not obey other mahouts. The mahout trained the elephant for twenty years. At age twenty, the elephant began to work. Elephants worked for about thirty-five years. They stopped work at age fifty-five or sixty—like people.

Today, most elephants and mahouts have no work. But the elephants are still very important in Thailand. Visitors to Thailand want to see them. The Thai people are very proud of their elephants.

象夫负责训练、喂养、照顾大象，这是一项很辛苦的工作。一头大象一天需要550磅（250公斤）植物和80加仑（300升）水，每天早上得接受6小时的训练。大象和象夫熟悉后，能辨认出象夫的声音和气味，还能听懂他的指示。大象对自己的象夫很顺从，但它不会听从别的象夫的指令。大象在接受象夫20年的训练后便开始工作，一般工作35年左右，就像人一样，他们通常在55或60岁时退休。

现在，大多数大象和象夫都无事可做。但在泰国，大象仍然很重要，因为到泰国观光的游客都想一睹大象的风采。泰国人民也为本国的大象感到自豪。

---

get used to 习惯于   instruction *n.* 指示；用法说明

12

How Did Rich Romans Live?

Over 2,000 years ago, there were many rich people in Rome. The Roman government controlled a lot of land. They *controlled* most of Europe. The Romans *forced* everyone to use Roman customs. Everyone paid Roman taxes and *obeyed* Roman laws. The government workers had to speak Latin. Latin was the language of Rome.

富有的罗马人是如何生活的?

两千年前，罗马有很多富人。罗马政府占有大片土地，他们控制了欧洲的大部分地区，并强迫那里的人民遵从罗马的习俗。每个人都得向罗马政府交税并遵守罗马的法律。政府工作人员必须使用拉丁语，拉丁语是罗马的母语。

control *v.* 控制
obey *v.* 服从；顺从

force *v.* 强制；强加

Rich Romans had two houses. They had one house in the country and one house in the city. The houses had many rooms. There was a garden in the middle. The floors and walls had beautiful *tiles*. Artists painted pictures on the tiles. The houses had water, a kitchen, and heating. Most people at that time didn't have these things. Many rich Romans had *slaves*. The slaves cooked and cleaned. Romans took men, women, and children from other countries to work as slaves.

The Romans ate three meals a day. They ate the main meal in the afternoon. They ate for *several* hours. Rich families asked friends to come over for a big meal. They had special foods, like mice, oysters, and peacock. They ate with their fingers or a spoon. During meals, Romans didn't sit on chairs. They lay on sofas!

Most Romans went to public baths. They *relaxed* and met friends there. They swam in the pools, read, ate, and got a haircut. There

富有的罗马人有两套房子，在乡村和城市各一套。每套房屋都有很多个房间，房屋中央是花园，地板和墙壁都由美丽的瓦片构成，工匠们还在瓦片上绘上各种图画。房屋里有厨房及供水、供暖设备，这在当时并不多见。很多有钱的罗马人都使用奴隶做饭和清洁房屋，这些奴隶都是从国外来的男人，妇女，也包括孩子。

罗马人一天吃三顿饭，下午是主餐，要吃好几个小时。富有人家一般会邀请朋友过来聚餐，他们会吃一些特殊的食物，例如，老鼠，牡蛎和孔雀。罗马人吃饭时用手指或者用羹匙，用餐期间他们躺在沙发上而不是坐在椅子上。

大多数罗马人都去公共浴池，在那里他们可以很放松，也可与一些朋友会面。他们在池子里游泳，看书，吃饭和剪发。那里一般有三种洗浴方

tile *n.* 瓦片　　　　　　　　　slave *n.* 奴隶
several *pron.* 几个　　　　　　relax *v.* 使放松

were three kinds of baths: very cold, warm, and hot. Romans cleaned their bodies in another way. They rubbed *olive* oil on their bodies. Then they took it off with a knife. They believed clean people were very healthy.

Rich Romans were always clean. The men shaved their face hair and had short haircuts. Some men *dyed* their hair black. Women had long hair and wore makeup. They put powder on their faces and put color on their lips. The Romans also wanted to smell clean. They used a lot of perfume. They used different perfumes for different parts of their bodies. They put perfume on their furniture, clothes, and horses, too.

The rich Romans had interesting lives. Today we use many things from the Romans, such as perfume, glass windows, and even *ketchup*!

式：冷水浴，温水浴和热水浴。罗马人还有其他方式清洁身体。他们把橄榄油涂抹在身上，再用小刀刮掉。他们认为干净的人会拥有健康。

富有的罗马人都很爱干净。男人刮脸，留短发，一些男人还把头发染成黑色。妇女都留长发，化妆。她们用粉擦脸并在嘴唇上涂上颜色。罗马人希望自己闻起来很清爽，都用香水。在身体的不同部分使用不同类型的香水，他们还把香水喷在家具，衣服和马身上。

富有的罗马人的生活非常有趣。今天我们使用的香水，玻璃窗和调味番茄酱都是从那时的罗马人那儿延续来的。

---

olive *n.* 橄榄   dye *v.* 染

ketchup *n.* 番茄酱

13

Who Is the Most Important Person from History?

What person from history has the greatest *effect* on our lives today? Recently, a group of many different *experts* decided it was a man named Johann Gutenberg. Gutenberg is famous for inventing printing, but he didn't really *invent* it. He invented a better way of printing.

谁是历史上最重要的人？

谁是历史上对我们今天生活影响最大的人？最近，一组来自不同领域的专家们得出结论，这个人的名字叫作约翰·谷登堡。他因发明了印刷术而闻名，但实际上他并不是发明了印刷术，只是发明了一种更好的印刷方法。

effect *n.* 影响　　　　　　　　　　　　　　expert *n.* 专家
invent *v.* 发明

For hundreds of years people used blocks of wood to print. They used a knife to cut words in the block of wood. They made the words *backward*. Then they covered the block with ink and pressed it onto paper. When they pulled the paper from the inky blocks, the words appeared on the paper in the right direction. In Korea and China, people printed with metal stamps instead of wood. Either way, printing was difficult and very slow. People usually wrote books by hand, so it took several years to make one copy of a book.

Books were very expensive and *rare*. Only rich people could buy them, and only rich people could read. As more people learned to read, books became more popular. People around the world wanted to find a quicker, better, and less expensive way to print books. One of these people was Johann Gutenberg.

Gutenberg was born in Mainz, Germany, around 1400. We do not

数百年来人们都用木板进行印刷。他们用刀在圆木上刻出文字，这时的文字是反的。然后人们把墨汁涂在木板上，再把木板按在纸上，把纸揭下之后纸上的字就是正面的了。在中国和朝鲜，人们用铁板代替木板进行印刷。然而无论哪种方式，印刷速度都很慢而且很困难。人们通常用手抄写书籍，所以复制一本书通常需要几年的时间。

那时书籍非常昂贵和稀少，只有富人们可以购买和阅读。随着越来越多的人学习阅读，书籍变得更加普遍。全世界的人都想找到一种更快更好且更便宜的方式印制图书。约翰·谷登堡就是其中之一。

约翰·谷登堡于1400年左右生于德国的美因茨，具体年份我们无从

---

backward *adj.* 倒的；相反的　　　　　　rare *adj.* 稀罕的；珍贵的

know the exact year. He was an intelligent man, and he was good at working with metal. Gutenberg probably had no idea how people printed in China. His idea was to make a metal stamp for each letter of the alphabet and use the letters *over and over*. He could put the stamps together to make words and *arrange* the words to make pages. With ink on the stamps, he could press paper on them to make a page. A "printing press" machine could make hundreds of copies of a single page quickly. After that page, he could rearrange the same letters to make other words and print other pages.

It took Gutenberg many years to make the stamps for each letter of the alphabet. When he finished the stamps, he didn't have enough money to make the printing press. He borrowed money from a man named Johann Fust. They became business partners. After many years, Gutenberg's printing press was ready. Gutenberg printed his

---

考究。他非常聪明，擅长机械制造。约翰·谷登堡对中国的印刷术几乎一无所知，他认为给字母表的每一个字母制作一个模板，这样就可以重复使用，还可以把字母的模板组合在一起形成单词进而组合成文章。在模板上涂上墨水再盖上纸就可以了。一台这样的机器可以快速地印出数百页，然后他可以重排字母组合成其他的单词和文章。

约翰·谷登堡花了很多年时间为字母表的每个字母制作了模板。当他制作完成之后，他的钱已经不够用来制造印刷机。他从一名叫作约翰·福斯特的人手中借来资金，于是他们变成了商业合作伙伴。很多年后，约翰的印刷机终于一切就绪了，1455年左右，他印制了第一部书——《圣经》。

---

over and over 反复；再三　　　　　　　　arrange *v.* 安排；排列

first book, *the Bible*, around 1455.

Johann Fust was a good businessman. He understood the importance of Gutenberg's invention. He took Gutenberg to *court* because Gutenberg still *owed* him money. Gutenberg had no money, so Fust took his printing press and started his own business. He printed and sold more Bibles and kept all the money. Gutenberg was sad and broke. He died in 1468, a poor man.

Today people remember Johann Gutenberg. The city of Mainz has a *statue* of him and a museum. His *original* printing press is in the museum. They print several pages a day to show that it is still in good condition. There are only forty-eight copies of the original Bible. It is the most expensive book in the world. In 1987, a Gutenberg Bible sold in New York for $5.3 million.

　　约翰·福斯特是一个精明的商人。他明白谷登堡这项发明的重要性。由于谷登堡一直欠他的钱，他把谷登堡告上了法庭，但谷登堡没有能力还款，于是福斯特拿走了他的印刷机并开始了自己的生意。他印刷并销售圣经，独吞了所有的利润。谷登堡非常悲伤，他破产了，并于1468年死去，去世时一贫如洗。

　　今天的人仍然怀念约翰·谷登堡。美因茨城为他建了一座纪念馆和一尊雕塑，他制作的印刷机至今仍在博物馆展出。人们每天仍用它进行少量印刷以示印刷机的状况依旧良好。最初的圣经如今只有48本，是世界上最昂贵的书籍。1987年，一本约翰·谷登堡印刷的圣经在美国纽约卖到了530万美元。

---

court *n.* 法庭　　　　　　　　owe *v.* 欠

statue *n.* 雕像　　　　　　　original *adj.* 最初的；原先的

What Are Fattening Rooms?

In North America and Europe, most women want to be *slim*. In those places, a slim woman is a beautiful woman. People think that a slim woman is *healthy* and careful about what she eats. But in some parts of the world, women want to be fat. In many parts of Africa,

何谓增肥室?

在北美及欧洲，大多数妇女都渴望苗条的身材。因为在这些地方，苗条的身材是美丽的象征。人们认为苗条的女人是健康的，注意饮食的。但在世界的其他一些地方，女人们却想变得肥胖。例如在非洲的许多地方，胖女人被视为美丽的女人。多胖才算胖呢？没有统一

slim *adj.* 苗条的；纤细的   healthy *adj.* 健康的

a fat woman is a beautiful woman. How fat? There is no *limit*. If a woman is fat, they think that she is healthy and rich. If she is slim, that means she is a worker with little money and not enough food to eat. Also, people believe that a slim woman will be sick or that she can't have children. A fat woman has enough food to eat, so she is healthy and will have many healthy babies.

To help girls and women look healthy and beautiful, people in central Africa send them to a fattening room. Fattening rooms are an old *tradition* and an important part of a girl's life. After a girl goes to a fattening room, her family and her village say that she is a woman. The fattening room is usually near the family's house or part of it. In the fattening room, a girl sits on a special chair until it is time to eat. Then she sits on the floor on a *mat* made of leaves. She also sleeps on the floor. Her mother gives her bowls of food like rice, yams, and

---

的标准。如果一个女人很胖，人们便认为她健康而富有。如果她很苗条，那代表她是个工人，没有钱也没有足够的东西吃。同样，人们认为瘦女人是病态的而且不能生育后代。胖女人有足够的食物吃，所以她是健康的并能生很多孩子。

为使女人看起来健康而美丽，生活在中非的人们把她们送进增肥室。进增肥室是一项古老的传统，也是每个女孩生命中非常重要的一部分。当一个女孩进过增肥室之后，她的家人及同乡才会把她称作是真正的女人。增肥室通常离家很近或者就在家里。在增肥室中，女孩通常坐在特制的椅子上，定时进餐；也会坐在草编成的垫子上，睡觉也在地板上。她的母亲

---

limit *n.* 界限；限制   tradition *n.* 传统
mat *n.* 垫子

beans—the kinds of foods that help her get fat. She also drinks a lot of water.

In the fattening room, the girl does not move very much. She can only eat, sleep, and get fatter. Her only *visitors* are women who teach her how to sit, walk, and talk in front of her future husband. They also give her advice about cleaning, sewing, and cooking. It is boring to be in the fattening room for so long with nothing to do, but the girl doesn't mind. She knows that it is important for her.

In southeastern Nigeria, brides go to a fattening room or a fattening farm before they get married. They cannot leave the farm for many weeks. At the end of this time, but before the wedding, the brides walk through the village so everyone can *admire* their big bodies. After a woman is married, she can also go to a fattening room. She may go several times because it is important for her to

---

会在碗中给她盛上米饭、甘薯、豆类等作为食物——这些都是使人发胖的食物，同时她也会喝很多水。

在增肥室内的女孩通常不怎么活动，她们只有吃饭和睡觉，然后长胖，唯一的探访者就是那些教她们怎么在未来的丈夫面前端坐、行走和讲话的女人，同样她们也会给她关于如何清洁房间、缝纫和烹饪方面的建议。在增肥室内长时间无所事事是令人厌烦的，但女孩们通常不介意。她们知道这很重要。

在尼日利亚东南部，新娘在出嫁前要进增肥室或增肥农场，她们要在那里待上几星期。在婚礼之前，新娘穿过村庄以便让人们羡慕她们那丰满的身材。妇女结婚后同样可以回到增肥室。她们可以往返多次，因为保持

---

visitor n. 访问者；参观者　　　　　admire v. 钦佩；羡慕

stay fat. A man wants his wife to be fat so other people will think that the man is rich and that he is a *responsible* man.

If parents don't send their daughter to a fattening room, their friends and *relatives* may laugh at them. They will say that the parents are not doing their duty. In the old days, girls sometimes stayed in a fattening room for two years. Today some families cannot afford more than a few months. Also, fattening rooms are not very popular in cities now. In cities, health education and Western culture have a big effect on people's ideas. But in villages, this traditional custom continues.

In Niger, they have a festival to celebrate the heaviest woman. Here, women have a *contest* to see who is the fattest. On the morning of the contest, the women eat *enormous* amounts of food and drink lots of water. The fattest woman is the winner. She gets a prize—more food!

肥胖对她们来说具有很重要的意义。男人们都希望自己的妻子肥胖，这样别人就会认为他很富有并且很负责任。

如果父母没有送女儿去增肥室，朋友和亲戚就会笑话他们，说他们没有尽到责任。在过去，一些女孩有时会在增肥室待上两年。现在许多家庭最多让女孩在那里呆几个月，在城市中增肥室已经不是那么普遍。健康教育和西方文化已经在很大程度上影响了城市人的观念。但是在乡村，这种传统仍在延续。

在尼日尔，有一个专门的节日为体重最重的女人庆贺。这里的女人通过比赛来选出最胖的一个。比赛当天早晨，妇女们会吃大量的食物并饮大量的水。最胖的女人便是获胜者，赢得的奖品是——更多的食物。

---

responsible *adj.* 负责的
contest *n.* 竞赛；比赛

relative *n.* 亲戚
enormous *adj.* 巨大的；庞大的

15

Where Do People Celebrate Girls' Day and Boys' Day?

People in every country love their children. They *celebrate* them on their birthdays or name days. In Japan, there are *national* festivals to celebrate their children at the same time. These festivals are called Girls' Day and Boys' Day.

Girls' Day is also called the Doll Festival. The Japanese celebrate it on March 3 (the

---

哪里的人们庆祝女孩节和男孩节？

所有的父母都喜爱他们的孩子，在孩子的生日或起名日人们会举行庆祝仪式。在日本，有国家法定的节日来为孩子们庆祝。这些节日被称为女孩节或男孩节。

女孩节也称玩偶节，在日本通常是在3月3日（第三个月的第三

---

celebrate *v.* 庆祝   national *adj.* 国家的；民族的

45

third day of the third month). On this day, a girl's parents prepare a table in the best room in the house. They put a red cloth on the table. Then they put steps on the table. They arrange a set of fifteen special dolls on the steps. Each doll has its place on the steps. The dolls *represent* the royal family in ancient Japan—emperors, empresses, ministers, and famous musicians. The emperor and empress are on the top step.

These are not dolls for children to play with. They are expensive. An inexpensive set of dolls can cost $200. The most popular sets cost about $700. The prices can go up to thousands of dollars. Many grandparents buy a set of dolls for their first granddaughter. When they have more granddaughters, they buy other things to put with the table, such as small pieces of *furniture*. Some families buy one or

天）。这一天，女孩的父母在家中最好的屋子里准备一张桌子，在桌上铺上红布然后放上台阶。他们在台阶上放上15个不同的玩偶，每个玩偶都有自己的位置。玩偶代表日本的皇族——皇帝、皇后、大臣、著名的音乐家。皇帝与皇后在最高的台阶上。

这些玩偶不是用来给孩子们玩的。他们非常昂贵，便宜的一套也要200美元，最流行的一套要700美元，有的价格甚至可能高达上千美元。许多祖父母为他们的第一个外孙女购买整套的玩偶。当他们有了更多的外孙女时，他们买来更多的东西放在桌子上，比如说小件的家具，也有一些家庭每年只买一到两件家具或玩偶来增加他们的收藏。

represent *v.* 代表　　　　　　　　　　　　furniture *n.* 家具

two pieces of furniture or dolls each year to add to their *collection*.

In the festival, many girls wear the traditional *kimono*. They have parties with their friends and eat rice cakes and drink a special rice wine. The wine has no alcohol in it, so children can drink it. After the party, the family has a traditional dinner for the girls in the family.

Two months after Girls' Day, on May 5, the Japanese celebrate Boys' Day. Today they call it Children's Day. People fly *banners* on their houses. The banners are made of paper or cloth, and they look like fish. When the wind blows, the fish fill with air and seem to be swimming. Each family puts up one fish for each boy. The fish of the oldest boy is the largest, and it is on top. The youngest boy has the smallest fish at the bottom. These banners represent a type of fish called the carp. The carp is a strong and brave fish. It swims up the river against great difficulties and doesn't *give up*. People hope the

---

　　节日期间，女孩们穿上传统的和服。她们和朋友聚会，吃米糕饮米酒。这种酒不含酒精，所以儿童也可以喝。聚会结束后，每个家庭会为家里的女孩准备一顿传统的晚餐。

　　女孩节结束后的两个月，即5月5日，日本会庆祝男孩节，现在也称作儿童节。人们在自己的房子上挂上条幅，通常由纸或布制成，呈鱼状。风吹起来的时候里面会充满了空气，像是在游泳。每个家庭都会为家中的男孩挂一条鱼，最大的男孩的鱼也最大，并且放在最顶端。最小的男孩鱼也最小，放在最底端。这种条幅代表的是鲤鱼，因为鲤鱼是一种强壮而勇敢的鱼。它会逆流而上，不惧艰险，永不放弃。人们希望男孩们长大后能

---

collection *n.* 收藏；征集
banner *n.* 横幅

kimono *n.* 和服
give up 放弃

boys will grow to be strong and brave like the carp.

Inside the house, in a place everyone can see, there are Boys' Day dolls. These dolls represent famous soldiers and heroes in history. The boys sometimes wear *costumes* of soldiers, too. Rich families may put out old family *souvenirs*. They may also put out swords. The iris is an important flower on Boys' Day because its leaves look like a sword. They put iris leaves around the table with the dolls. They also add iris leaves to a hot bath. They believe that when you take a bath with iris leaves, it will protect you from sickness.

Japanese children are very happy on Girls' Day and Boys' Day, and they love these celebrations for many reasons. But the biggest reason is because there is no school!

像鲤鱼一样强壮和勇敢。

在家中一个明显的位置，摆放男孩节的玩偶，这些玩偶代表历史上最著名的英雄与士兵，男孩们有时也会穿士兵的服装。富裕的家庭可能会陈列出家族的纪念物，有时他们也会把剑摆出来。男孩节上鸢花是一种重要的花，因为它的叶子看起来像剑。他们把鸢花的叶子和玩偶摆在桌子的四周，还把叶子加入热的洗澡水中，他们也认为用鸢花的叶子洗澡会让你远离疾病。

日本的孩子们在女孩节和男孩节的时候非常快乐，他们有很多的理由喜爱这些庆祝活动。但最重要的原因是这一天不用上学！

---

costume *n.* 装束；服装   souvenir *n.* 纪念品

16

Why Is Marco Polo Famous?

Marco Polo was not the first European to travel to China, but he was the first to write about his travels. At that time, China was an unknown and *romantic* land to Europeans. Some people didn't *believe* it was a real place. Marco Polo helped them see the world as a much bigger and more interesting place.

为什么马可·波罗如此出名？

马可·波罗并不是第一个到中国旅行的欧洲人，但他却是第一个把经历写在游记上的人。在那个时代，对于欧洲人来说中国是一片神秘而浪漫的土地，许多人甚至不相信中国是真实存在的。是马可·波罗帮助他们认识到了这世界的广阔和有趣。

romantic *adj.* 浪漫的   believe *v.* 相信

Marco Polo was born in Venice in 1254. His father, Niccolo Polo, was a businessman and traveled away from home often. In 1265, Marco's father and uncle, Maffeo, decided to go to China. They were the first Europeans to travel there. In China, they met the emperor, Kublai Khan. The emperor thought the Europeans were interesting and invited them to return. The brothers went back to Italy and told Marco about their *adventures*. The brothers wanted to return to China, and this time they took seventeen-year-old Marco with them.

The three men left again for China in 1271. China was thousands of miles away from Venice. First they went by ship to the Mediterranean *coast* of Turkey. Then they went on land and passed through what is today Iran and Afghanistan. They crossed deserts and mountains and rivers. They had to travel for three years.

When they finally reached China, the emperor Kublai Khan welcomed his old friends and the young man with them. Marco was a

---

马可·波罗于1254年生在威尼斯，他的父亲尼阁·波罗是一名商人，经常外出经商。1265年，马可·波罗的父亲和叔父马法罗决定去中国，他们是最早去那里旅行的一批欧洲人。在中国他们见到了皇帝忽必烈，皇帝认为欧洲人很有趣并邀请他们以后再回来。兄弟俩返回意大利后对马可·波罗讲述了他们在中国的经历，并决定重返中国，这次他们把17岁的马可·波罗也带上了。

三人于1271年开始出发，中国距威尼斯有千里之遥，他们首先乘船到了地中海沿岸的土耳其，然后上岸穿越了如今的伊朗和阿富汗，他们穿越沙漠、高山和河流，走了近三年。

当他们到达中国后，忽必烈热情地接待了他的老朋友和这位年轻人。

---

adventure *n.* 冒险

coast *n.* 海岸

good student of languages, and soon he learned Chinese. Kublai Khan liked Marco Polo and gave him a job. He traveled all over the country to represent the emperor. Marco saw beautiful things and met many people. He wrote about all of this later. The Polos had a good life in China, but after seventeen years there, they wanted to return to Italy.

In Italy, Marco couldn't *settle down*. He became the *captain* of a ship because he wanted to continue his travels. Soon Venice went to war with Genoa, another Italian city. Marco and his ship joined the war. Venice lost, and Marco Polo became a prisoner in Genoa.

Marco shared his room in the prison with a man named Rustichello da Pisa. They passed the time by talking about their lives. Polo talked about his travels and his life in China. Rustichello loved Polo's stories. He was a writer, so he helped Marco write down his stories in a book. The title of the book in English is *The Travels of Marco Polo*.

马可·波罗是个学习语言的好手，他很快就掌握了汉语。忽必烈很喜欢他，并赐给他一个职位，这样他就可以代表皇帝巡视全国。马可·波罗游览了很多地方也结交了很多人，日后他把这些都写进了游记里。马可·波罗家族在中国生活得很愉快，但17年后，他们决定返回意大利。

在意大利，马可·波罗并没有安顿下来，因为想继续自己的旅行，他当上了一艘船的船长。不久威尼斯陷入了与意大利热那亚的战争，马可·波罗和他的船也卷入了战争。威尼斯沦陷了，马可·波罗也成了热那亚的俘虏。

在狱中，马可·波罗与一个名叫鲁斯蒂切罗的人关押在一起，他们谈论过去的生活来消磨时光。马可·波罗讲述了他在中国的旅行与生活。鲁斯蒂切罗很喜欢马可·波罗的故事，身为作家，他帮助马可·波罗把他的

---

settle down 定居；平静下来   captain *n.* 船长

In the book, Polo *describes* the cities he saw, the people he met, and the way people lived. He describes animals, plants, and things that people used. He describes paper money, gunpowder, and *porcelain* vases. People in Europe didn't know about these things. They didn't want to believe that the world was so different in other places. They said Marco Polo's stories were not true. They called him "Il Milione," the man of a million lies. Before he died in 1324, Marco Polo said, "I didn't write about half of the things that I saw." He knew no one believed him.

It took a long time, but people finally learned that Marco Polo's stories were mostly true. Many explorers used Polo's book as a *guide*. Christopher Columbus read it before he made his first trip to the New World.

故事写成一本书，书的名字就叫作《马可·波罗游记》。

书中，马可·波罗描述了他游览过的城市，他遇到的人以及那些人的生活方式。他描述了动植物和人们的生活日用品，他同样还描述了纸币、火药以及瓷器花瓶等。欧洲人不懂这些东西，他们不愿相信世界的另外一部分是如此的不同。他们说马可·波罗的故事是虚假的，把他称作"百万谎言骗子"。1324年，马可·波罗临终前说："我只写出了我见到的东西的一少半"，但他知道没人会相信他。

过了很长时间，人们终于认识到了马可·波罗的故事的真实性。许多探险者以马可·波罗的书作为指导。克里斯托福·哥伦布在开始他的新世界之旅前就读过这本书。

---

describe *v.* 描述；形容
guide *n.* 指导；向导

porcelain *n.* 瓷；瓷器

17

Who Reached the South Pole First?

In 1900, there were two places in the world that were not *explored*. These were lands of snow and ice— the North Pole and the South Pole.

As a young man in Norway, Roald Amundsen read about explorers who tried to reach the North Pole, and he wanted to reach it, too. It became his *dream*. The first step was to learn how

---

第一个到达南极的人是谁？

1900年时，世界上有两个地方还未曾被探索。他们是两个被冰雪覆盖的大陆——北极与南极。

一个叫罗尔德·亚孟森的挪威青年人读了探险者欲征服北极的故事，而那也正是他的梦想。第一步是学习如何航行，他22岁时在船上当了一名

---

explore *v.* 探索   dream *n.* 梦想

to sail, so Amundsen went to sea as a worker on a ship when he was twenty-two. Later, he worked on a ship that went to Antarctica. Antarctica is the coldest place on Earth. The South Pole is in the *center* of Antarctica. It was an exciting trip, but they did not reach the South Pole.

He sailed on many ships and worked his way up to the top jobs. In 1903, he was the captain of a ship on its way to the Arctic. This ship was the first to sail the Northwest Passage. The Northwest Passage was important because it helped people to travel from Europe to Asia.

Amundsen was now a famous explorer, and he started to plan his *voyage* to the North Pole. Then he learned that an American named Robert Peary was already there. Amundsen wanted to be first, so he changed his plans and went to the South Pole *instead*. He heard that an English explorer named Robert Scott was on his way to the South Pole,

---

船员。后来，他在一艘驶往南极洲的船上工作，南极洲是世界上最寒冷的地方，南极点是南极洲的中心。这是一次令人激动的旅行，但最终他们没能到达南极点。

他在许多船上工作过并慢慢升到了更高职位。1903年，他成为一艘驶往北极的船的船长。这艘船是第一艘航行西北航线的船。这是条很重要的航线，人们可以通过它完成从欧洲到亚洲的旅行。

罗尔德·亚孟森已经是位著名的探险者了，他开始计划他的北极之旅。这时他听说一个名叫罗伯特·帕里的美国人已经到达那里了。亚孟森想做开拓者，于是他改变了计划，改去南极。但他听说一个名叫罗伯特·斯科特的英国人也在去南极的路上，于是罗尔德·亚孟森让人给他送去消

---

center *n.* 中心　　　　　　　　　　　　　　　voyage *n.* 航行
instead *adv.* 代替；反而

so Amundsen sent him a message. He said that this was now a race.

When Amundsen reached Antarctica, he and four of his men started toward the South Pole. There was only ice and snow, and the wind was freezing. He had teams of dogs to pull *sleds* with food and tents. They climbed mountains of snow and fell through holes in the ice. Finally, they were near the South Pole. They didn't know whether Scott was already there. They reached the South Pole on December 14, 1911, and there was no *sign* of Scott. Amundsen won the race.

Scott and his group were on their way, but they were not prepared for the *extreme* weather. They did not have the right clothes, and Scott had horses instead of dogs. The horses were not used to the freezing weather of Antarctica, and the men had to shoot them. The men then had to carry everything. Scott and his men *finally* arrived at the South Pole, but thirty-three days after Amundsen's group. Scott saw the Norwegian flag and was sad. He and his men

---

息，说从现在开始要和他进行一次比赛。

当亚孟森到达南极洲后，他和四个随从向南极点进军。这里只有冰和雪，寒风刺骨，他们用狗拉着装满食物和帐篷的雪橇，在雪山和冰窟间艰难前行，最后终于靠近了南极。但他们不知道罗伯特·斯科特是否已经到了那里，当他们于1911年12月14日到达时，那里并没有罗伯特·斯科特的踪迹，他们赢得了比赛。

罗伯特·斯科特和他的伙伴也在路上，但他们没有做好应付极端恶劣天气的准备。他们既没有足够保暖的衣服，交通工具又是马而不是狗。马无法适应南极洲极端寒冷的天气，他们只好射死了马，亲自拿东西。罗伯特·斯科特最终也到达了南极，但那已经是亚孟森到达后的第三十三天了。罗伯特·斯科特看到了挪威国旗，非常悲伤，他和他的队伍开始返回

---

sled *n.* 雪橇

extreme *adj.* 极端的；极度的

sign *n.* 迹象

finally *adv.* 终于；最终

returned to their camp. On the way, one man died. At the camp the four men didn't have fuel for heat.

People around the world were very happy for Amundsen, but they wanted to know whether Scott and his men also reached the South Pole. They waited many months, but there was no news. The next summer, another group of people went to look for them. They finally found the camp and the bodies of Scott and his men in their tent. They were all frozen.

Amundsen reached the South Pole, but he still had the *goal* to go to the North Pole. In 1926, he and his friend Umberto Nobile flew in an airship over the North Pole—another first! A few years later, Nobile's airship crashed on another Arctic trip. Amundsen went to search for him. On the way, his airplane crashed, and the great explorer died. Other people found Nobile later—he *survived*.

营地。在路上一个伙伴死了，回到营地的四个人也没有燃料用来取暖。

全世界的人都在为罗尔德·亚孟森感到高兴，他们也想知道罗伯特·斯科特的团队是否也到了南极。人们等了几个月，仍旧没有消息。第二年夏天，另一队人开始寻找他们，最后人们在帐篷中找到了罗伯特·斯科特和他的伙伴们的尸体，已经被冻僵了。

罗尔德·亚孟森去过了南极，但他仍想去北极。1926年，他和他的朋友诺毕尔乘飞艇飞越了北极，这又是人类历史上的第一次！几年之后，诺毕尔的飞艇在一次北极圈之旅中坠毁，亚孟森出发去寻找他。在路上，亚孟森的飞艇坠毁了，伟大探险家的生命结束了。后来有人找到了诺毕尔，他活了下来。

---

goal *n.* 目的；目标

survive *v.* 幸免于；幸存

18

What Is the Royal Flying Doctor Service?

Most people in Australia live in cities on the *coast*. Very few people live in the huge middle area, and houses are far away from each other. Australians call this part of the country "the Outback." In the past, when people in the Outback had an accident or got sick, there were no doctors to take care of them. Today people in the Outback can call a special *service* called the

什么是皇家飞行医生服务？

大多数澳大利亚人都住在海滨城市，只有少数人住在空旷的中部地区，并彼此相距很远。澳大利亚人称这片地区为澳洲内陆。过去，在内陆生活的人即使发生交通事故或生病也没有医生来为他们治疗。今天生活在内陆里的人可以呼叫皇家飞行医生并在短短几分钟内就能得到救助。皇家飞行医生们乘飞机来到那些没有医疗保障的地区，为那里

coast *n.* 海岸   service *n.* 服务

Royal Flying Doctor Service and get help in a few minutes. The Royal Flying Doctors use airplanes to reach people in places that don't have doctors.

A *minister*, *Reverend* John Flynn, started the Flying Doctor Service in the 1920s. He traveled by truck through central and northern Australia for his church. Many times he saw people die because there was no doctor near. He thought, "There must be some way to help these people. First, I will build hospitals for them."

Flynn worked very hard, and by 1927 there were ten small hospitals in central and northern Australia. Nurses took care of the sick and *injured* people. But Flynn was not *satisfied*. He had hospitals and nurses, but he needed doctors. But how could doctors visit the people who lived far away in the Outback and could not go to a hospital? He had an idea! "The doctors can travel by airplane. We will also build a place for a plane to land near every Outback home."

的人服务。

　　约翰·弗林是一位受人尊敬的部长，在20世纪20年代创立了飞行医生服务队。他在乘坐卡车穿越澳大利亚中北部视察教堂时，多次亲眼看见人们因为附近没有医生，得不到治疗而死去。他想："必须要想办法帮助这些人。首先，我要为这些人修建医院。"

　　约翰·弗林工作非常努力，1927年在澳大利亚中部和北部就建起了10座小医院。护士们照顾生病和受伤的人们，但约翰·弗林并不满意。虽然有了医院与护士，但更需要医生。如何才能让医生为那些因住在偏僻地区而不能来医院的人服务呢？他有了主意！"医生们可以乘坐飞机，我们

---

minister *n.* 部长；大臣　　　　　　reverend *adj.* 值得尊敬的
injured *adj.* 受伤的　　　　　　　　satisfied *adj.* 满足的；满意的

Many people laughed at the idea. Airplane travel in 1927 was a new and dangerous thing.

There were other problems, too. How can people so far away ask for a doctor? Flynn said, "We will use a radio to send and *receive* messages." At that time, radios in the Outback could receive messages, but they could not send them. Flynn got in touch with a young radio engineer. The engineer agreed to help him. The engineer worked for three years and finally made a radio that could send and receive messages.

Everything was ready. The Flying Doctor Service began in May 1928. The Service was a great *success*, and Flynn was very happy. In the first year, doctors made fifty flights. They flew 18,000 miles, helped 225 people, and saved 4 lives. Flynn now wanted the Service to be in all parts of the Outback. His church did not have enough money for this plan, so the different states in Australia agreed to help. Each state built one or two hospitals.

也会修建场地，在任何地方都能自由起降。" 许多人对此嗤之以鼻，因为在1927年乘飞机旅行是一件新鲜而危险的事。

还有一些问题没有解决。其中之一就是居民如何呼叫医生？约翰·弗林说，"我们会用无线电来收发消息"。那时候，内陆的无线电设备只可以接收讯息但不能发送。约翰·弗林与另一位年轻的无线电工程师取得了联系，工程师答应帮助他。工程师经过3年的研究，终于解决了这个问题。

万事俱备后，飞行医生服务终于在1928年5月开始了。这项服务取得了巨大成功，约翰·弗林非常高兴。第一年，医生们飞行了50次，飞行距离近18,000公里，救助了225人，救了4条生命。约翰·弗林想把这项服务推广到内陆的所有地区，但他的教堂并没有足够的资金资助他，于是澳

---

receive *v.* 收到　　　　　　　　　　　success *n.* 成功

In 1942, the Flying Doctor Service *came up with* another good idea. Every home in the Outback got a prepared first-aid kit. Each kit had the same drugs, *bandages*, and other first-aid materials. Everything in the *kit* had its own special number. Later, the kits had a picture of a body with numbers for all the different parts. When people got sick or injured, they used the radio to call the medical center. The doctor asked about the problem by number. Then the doctor told the caller to use medicine from the kit by numbers, too. For example, the doctor said, "Take one pill from number 8 every three hours," or "Put number 22 on your injured leg."

Today there are 3,000 medical kits, 22 hospitals, and 40 Royal Flying Doctor Service airplanes. Each year, the service helps about 197,000 people.

大利亚的各个州纷纷给予帮助，几乎在每个州都建了一到两所医院。

　　1942年，飞行医生服务队提出了另一个好主意。内陆的每一个家庭都得到了一套急救药箱。每套药箱都有相同的药，绷带以及其他急救用品。药箱里的每一件用品都有自己的编码，而且，药箱附带了一张标有人体各部分代码的图示。当有人生病或受伤时，他们用无线电联系医疗中心，医生按照人体代码来询问病情，而后告诉患者按照急救药箱里药品的代码服药。比如，医生会说，"每3小时吃一片8号药"或者"把22号药敷在你的伤腿上"。

　　今天内陆有3000套急救药箱，22家医院和40架提供皇家飞行医生服务的飞机。每年通过这项服务大约197,000多人受到救助。

---

come up with 提出；拿出

kit *n.* 工具箱

bandage *n.* 绷带

How Did the Egyptians Make Mummies?

The ancient Egyptians *believed in* many gods. They also believed that their kings, called pharaohs, were gods. They believed that the pharaoh could help them even after he died. Because of this, they wanted the

埃及木乃伊是如何制作的?

古埃及人信仰许多神。他们也相信自己的国王，也称之为法老，就是神的意思。他们甚至相信法老在死后也会给他们带来帮助。因此，他们不仅希望法老在世的时候生活得很好，也希望法老死后也能生

believe in 信仰；信任

pharaoh to have a good life, and a good life after death, or afterlife. One way to give the pharaoh a good afterlife was to *preserve* his body. Egyptians believed this was important for the pharoah's spirit. This would help the spirit *recognize* the body. This is the reason the Egyptians made mummies.

As soon as a *pharaoh* died, the top priest, together with his helpers, started work on the body. They took out some of the organs but left the heart inside the body. They dried the organs and put them in special jars. Later they put the jars in the pharaoh's tomb, a special building for the dead. Next they took out the brain and threw it away. The Egyptians did not think the brain was important. On the outside of the body, they rubbed a kind of salt on the skin to help dry the body completely. This took about forty days. Then they filled the

---

活得好。方法之一就是保存他们的肉体。埃及人相信这对法老的灵魂很重要，能帮助法老的灵魂找到他的身体，这就是埃及人制作木乃伊的原因。

法老死后，大祭司及他的助手们开始对遗体进行加工。他们取出一些器官，只留下心脏。把这些器官晒干放到特制的坛子里，然后把坛子放进特别为法老修建的坟墓里。接下来取出大脑并将它丢掉，他们认为大脑不是很重要。在尸体的外部，他们在皮肤涂上盐以使尸体彻底干燥。这一过程需要用40天，然后用布和沙子填满身体以保持形状，再涂上油和香料，

---

preserve *v.* 保存；保持   recognize *v.* 认出；承认

pharaoh *n.* 法老

body with cloth and sand to keep its shape, rubbed it with oil and perfumes, and covered it with lots of wax. The Arabic word for wax is mum, so that's how we got the word mummy.

The pharaoh's body was now prepared. Next they wrapped it in very long pieces of cloth. Again, they used a lot of wax to make the pieces stick together. At last, after seventy days, the mummy was ready. They painted the face of the dead pharaoh on the mummy to help his spirit recognize him. The mummy then went into two or three coffins, one inside the other, and finally into the *tomb*.

During his lifetime, a pharaoh also prepared for the afterlife. He built his tomb, which took many years and a lot of hard work. The tomb was in the shape of a *pyramid*. The pointed top helped the pharaoh's spirit climb into the sky to join the gods who lived there. Each pharaoh tried to be greater than the one before, so

---

最后用蜡加以覆盖。阿拉伯语的蜡就是MUM，这就是mummy(木乃伊)这个词的来历。

法老尸体的准备工作已经就绪，下一步是用很长的布把尸体裹起来，再次用蜡把布加工得非常结实。70天之后木乃伊就制作好了。他们把死去法老的面容画在木乃伊上帮助法老的灵魂进行识别。木乃伊被装入两到三层的棺木中，一层套着另一层，最后放进坟墓。

在生前法老就已经在为死后的生活做准备了。他耗费大量时间和人力物力来为自己修建坟墓。坟墓呈金字塔状，尖顶能帮助法老的灵魂升上天空加入上苍的众神中。每个法老都想比前任法老更伟大，因此金字塔的修

---

tomb n. 坟墓

pyramid n. 金字塔

the pyramids got larger and larger. More than seventy pharaohs built pyramids for themselves. The Great Pyramid at Giza is still the largest stone *structure* in the world. The tomb was filled with everything the person needed for the afterlife, such as food, clothing, and jewelry. There were also model figures of men and women called shabtis. These figures became workers for the pharaoh in the afterlife. Some tombs had 365 shabtis, one for each day of the year.

Later other people such as priests, people in government, and rich Egyptians also wanted to be mummies so that they could join the pharaoh in the afterlife. They even made some animals such as cats, dogs, and birds into mummies because these animals represented gods.

When everything was in the tomb, they closed it very *tight*.

建也越来越宏伟。有70多位法老为自己修建了金字塔，吉萨大金字塔是世界上最庞大的石头建筑。坟墓中装满了人需要的一切，比如食物、衣物和珠宝。墓中还有男人和女人的雕像，称为"回答"（仆人）。这些雕像成为法老死后的仆人，有些坟墓拥有365个仆人，意味着法老在一年的每一天都有仆人。

后来，其他的神父、政府工作人员以及有钱的埃及人也想死后成为木乃伊，这样他们就能追随法老了。他们甚至制作了猫、狗以及鸟的木乃伊，因为他们认为这些动物能代表神。

一切就绪后，人们把坟墓牢牢封闭。埃及人相信法老的坟墓就是神灵

---

structure n. 结构；建筑物   tight adv. 紧紧地

Egyptians believed a pharaoh's tomb was like the house of a god. If someone entered it, terrible things would happen to that person—he or she could even die. But this did not stop people from entering the tombs. During *construction*, some workers built secret *tunnels* into the pyramids. Then they went in later to steal from them. Some coffins had special doors for the same reason. Thieves went into almost all the tombs. They stole *treasures* such as gold and jewelry.

Today, most of the treasures are lost or in museums, but the pyramids of Egypt are still there. Every year, thousands of tourists from around the world visit the pyramids and think of the pharaohs who built them. So in a way, the pharaohs reached their goal—they live on, at least through their tombs.

的家。如果有人擅自闯入，可怕的事情就会发生在他们头上——会死去。但这并不能阻止人们进入坟墓。在建筑过程中，有些工人偷偷修建了通入金字塔的秘密通道，以供随后秘密潜入进行盗窃。还有些棺椁也因同样的目的特制了入口。窃贼潜入过几乎所有的墓室，从中盗取金银财宝。

今天，大多数宝贝已经被盗或被陈列在博物馆中，但是埃及金字塔依然屹立不倒。每年，全世界成千上万的游客来参观金字塔并缅怀逝去的法老们。因而，在某种意义上法老们达到了他们的目的——继续活在世上，至少金字塔让人们记住了他们。

---

construction *n.* 建造；建设　　　　　　　　tunnel *n.* 隧道；地道
treasure *n.* 财宝；财富

Who Is Stephen Hawking?

There is a man driving around in a *motorized* wheelchair in Cambridge, England. He can only move his eyes and two fingers on his left hand. He *communicates* through a computer. He types words on the computer and the computer speaks for him. This man is Stephen

史蒂芬·霍金是谁?

在英国的剑桥,有一位以电动轮椅代步的人。他只能活动眼睛和左手上的两个指头,他靠一台计算机与人交流,他把单词键入计算机,由计算机扬声器替他讲话。这个人就是史蒂芬·霍金。他的勇气

---

motorized *adj.* 摩托化的   communicate *v.* 交流;交际

Hawking. People know him for his courage and his sense of humor. He is also the greatest physicist since Albert Einstein.

Stephen Hawking was born in 1942 in Oxford, England. His father was a *specialist* in *tropical* diseases. Stephen wanted to be a scientist too. He went to the University of Oxford and received a degree in physics. He then went to the University of Cambridge to study for a Ph.D. During this time doctors discovered that he had ALS, which is sometimes called Lou Gehrig's disease. This *fatal* disease weakens all of the body's muscles. Most people with ALS live for five years. The doctors thought Hawking would live for only two and a half more years. When Hawking heard this, he became very depressed.

At about this time he met Jane Wilde, a language student at

和幽默感家喻户晓，他也是继阿尔伯特·爱因斯坦之后最伟大的物理学家。

史蒂芬·霍金1942年生于英国的牛津。他的父亲是一位研究热带病的专家。史蒂芬也想当科学家，他到牛津大学读书，并获得了物理学学位。其后，他去剑桥大学攻读博士学位。在这期间，医生们发现他得了肌萎缩性脊髓侧索硬化症(ALS)，有时也叫卢伽雷病。这种致命的疾病使全身的肌肉萎缩，大多数得了ALS的人只能活5年。医生们认为，霍金只能再活两年半。他听到这个消息后，变得非常沮丧。

大约就在这个时候，霍金遇到了简·怀尔德——剑桥的一名学语言的

---

specialist *n.* 专家   tropical *adj.* 热带的
fatal *adj.* 致命的

Cambridge. They fell in love and got married in 1965. Hawking has often said that his wife gave him the courage to continue to study and work. Although Hawking had become more severely *paralyzed*, he became a professor at Cambridge. Luckily, the work of a physicist only requires one thing: the mind. Hawking had a son and then a daughter. He had another son 12 years later when his disease had gotten much worse. His youngest son has never heard his father's real voice. He has only heard the voice from the computer.

Hawking does research about how the *universe* began. He sees connections and works out explanations that other people cannot. His research has influenced many other scientists. Some of his ideas are so advanced that other scientists cannot prove them yet. His most famous ideas are about black holes. Black holes are not

学生。他们相爱了，并于1965年结婚。霍金常说，他妻子给了他继续学习和工作的勇气。虽然霍金的瘫痪越来越严重，但他仍成了剑桥的教授。幸运的是，一位物理学家的工作只需要一种东西：头脑。霍金相继有了一儿一女，12年后，当他的病情更加恶化时，他又有了一个儿子。他的小儿子从来没有听到过父亲真正的声音，他只能听到从计算机里传出的父亲的话语。

霍金从事宇宙起源的研究。他看到了宇宙中的联系，并做出了其他人作不出来的解释，他的研究影响了许多别的科学家。他的一些想法很超

paralyzed *adj.* 瘫痪的；麻痹的   universe *n.* 宇宙

really holes. They are areas in space that are very *dense*. They are so dense that even light cannot pass through. That is why they are called black holes.

As his disease got worse, money became a problem for Stephen Hawking. He had a lot of medical expenses. He needed special wheelchairs, nurses 24 hours a day, and machines to help him read and speak. To earn extra money, Hawking gave speeches and published articles. Then someone told him to write a book that explained the universe to ordinary people. Hawking agreed and wrote *A Brief History of Time*. The book sold over 8 million copies worldwide, and Hawking became a millionaire. Even though most people could not understand Hawking's ideas, he *amazed* them. Hawking became world famous. He met the Queen of England, he

---

前，以至于其他科学家们还证明不了。霍金最著名的思想就是黑洞理论。黑洞并不是真正的洞，它们是宇宙中密度很大的区域，其密度大得连光都透不过去。这就是称之为黑洞的原因。

　　由于他的病情越来越恶化，所以对于史蒂芬·霍金来说，钱便成了问题。他的医疗费用很高，他需要特制的轮椅、一天24小时的护理以及帮助他阅读和说话的机器。为了多挣钱，霍金演讲并发表文章。后来，有人建议他写书，向普通人解释宇宙问题。霍金同意了，写出了《时间简史》。该书在全世界售出了800万册，于是，霍金成了百万富翁。尽管大多数人

---

dense *adj.* 密集的；浓厚的　　　　　　　　amaze *v.* 使惊奇

was on the covers of magazines, and he appeared on television shows.

In 1990, Hawking ended his 25-year marriage. This was shocking to many of his friends because his wife, Jane, was very *devoted* to him. She took care of all of his needs. She fed him, bathed him, dressed him, and raised their children by herself. Hawking left her for a younger woman—his nurse! They were married in 1995.

Hawking's strong personality and spirit have helped him to live with ALS for over 30 years. He has helped to make people aware of ALS and other disabilities. Hawking teaches us that even though a person is physically *disabled*, the mind has no limits.

理解不了霍金的思想，但他让人们感到惊奇，因此霍金闻名全世界。他见到了英国女王，他成了杂志封面人物，他也出现在电视节目中。

1990年，霍金结束了他25年的婚姻。这使许多朋友震惊，因为他的妻子简对他非常忠贞。简关照他的所有需要，给他喂饭，给他洗澡，帮他穿衣服，还自己带孩子。霍金离开她，是因为一位更年轻的女子——他的护士！两人于1995年结婚。

霍金坚强的个性和精神使得他能够与ALS抗争长达三十多年。他帮助人们认识了ALS以及其他的一些残疾病症。霍金教会了我们：尽管一个人会在身体上患有残废，但心灵无极限。

---

devoted *adj.* 忠诚的；献身……的　　　　　　　disabled *adj.* 残废的

21

What Does Hair Tell Us About People?

Throughout history, hair has always been used to make a fashion statement. It also tells us a lot about culture. In almost all societies, people have cut or styled their hair for practical or *decorative* reasons. For example, the ancient Greeks liked blond hair, so both men and women lightened their hair. On the other hand, the Romans preferred dark hair, and Saxon men are seen in paintings to have hair and beards of blue, green, bright red, and orange. The Assyrian *culture* made an art of hairstyling.

头发向我们揭示了有关人的什么奥秘？

在人类历史长河中，头发一直是引领潮流的主要因素。同样，通过它我们也能解读文化。几乎在每个社会里，人们都会出于实用或装饰的原因修剪或设计发型。例如，古代希腊人喜欢金黄色的头发，他们都把头发染亮。而罗马人喜欢黑发；撒克逊人喜欢用涂料把头发和胡须染成蓝色、绿色、鲜红色和橙色。亚述文化把发型设计看成一门艺术。

decorative *adj.* 装饰的   culture *n.* 文化

People curled, oiled, and perfumed their hair; they also cut their hair and beards in layers to look like pyramids. Assyrian soldiers needed to have their hair properly curled before they went to war. The Assyrian people used hairstyles to show their position and employment. Assyrian women of high rank, as well as women in Egypt, put on fake beards at meetings to show authority.

Hair is often a sign of *superiority*. Primitive men put bones, feathers, and other objects in their hair to impress and *intimidate* their enemies. Later, the Romans made the people they conquered cut off their hair to show *submission*. In seventeenth century China, Manchu men shaved the front of the hair and combed the hair in the back into a braided tail. They also made those they conquered wear this style.

Some cultures consider hair to be a *sensuous* object. For some people, not having hair or not showing it to others is a sign of religious

---

人们可以把头发烫卷、抹油或香熏。他们还把头发和胡须剪成塔状。亚述士兵在征战前必须把头发卷好。亚述人通过发型来表示他们的地位和工作。亚述和埃及上层妇女举行会议时戴上假胡须以显示她们的权威。

头发通常是权威的象征，原始人把骨头、羽毛和其他物品嵌入头发来威吓敌人，给他们留下深刻印象。后来罗马人让被征服者把头发剪掉以示归顺。在17世纪的中国，满族人把头前面的头发都剃光，后面的头发梳成辫子。他们还让被征服者也梳这个发型。

有的文化认为头发是一种感官的东西，对有些人来说，不留发或不展示自己头发是对宗教的一种虔诚。基督教徒和佛教徒都把头发剃光以表示

---

superiority *n.* 权威　　　　　　　intimidate *v.* 威吓；胁迫
submission *n.* 投降；服从　　　　sensuous *adj.* 刺激感官的

devotion. Christian and Buddhist monks often shave their heads to show *holiness* and retirement from the world. Many Christian nuns cover their hair. Some Muslim women cover their hair when they are in public, and men in certain countries wear a turban or head cloth for religious reasons.

In ancient and modern times, hair has been used to reveal a person's *emotions*, marital status, or age. For example, ancient Egyptian men and women usually shaved their hair. However, when they were in mourning, they grew it long. Hindu women, on the other hand, cut off their long hair as a sign of mourning. In medieval Europe, unmarried women showed their long hair in public, whereas married women covered theirs. Today, brides in the Maasai tribe in Africa have their heads shaved as part of their marriage ceremony, and mothers in the tribe shave their sons' hair when the boys become *adolescents*. Today, teenagers all over the world *demonstrate*

他们的圣洁和远离世俗。许多基督教徒把头发蒙起来。在公众场合，穆斯林妇女会把头发蒙起来。在有些国家，男人也会出于某种宗教原因戴上头巾或头布。

从古至今，头发可以表示人的情感、婚姻状况或年龄。比如，古埃及人喜欢剪发，但当他们参加追悼会时就会留长发。相反，印度人参加追悼会时要剪掉长发。在中世纪的欧洲国家，未出嫁的女孩在公众场合展示她们的长发，而婚后的妇女就必须将头发蒙起来。现今，非洲马塞部落的新娘把剃头当作她们婚礼的一个内容。这个部落的母亲会在儿子成年时给他们剃头。当今，世界的青年人都喜欢通过发型和头发颜色来展现他们的青春和个性。在

---

holiness *n.* 神圣

adolescent *n.* 青少年

emotion *n.* 情感

demonstrate *v.* 证明；展示

their youth and *individuality* through haircuts or hair colors. Even in countries like China and Japan, where dyed hair is considered untraditional, up to 68 percent of women and 20 percent of men—most of them young—now use hair color to reflect their individual personalities.

Wigs have always been popular as fashion statements and as signs of wealth or status. Ancient Egyptians shaved their heads for cleanliness and then covered their heads with wigs. The higher the status of a person, the bigger his or her wig was. Cleopatra wore different styles and colors of wigs, and another Egyptian queen wore such a heavy wig on important *occasions* that attendants had to help her walk. Queen Elizabeth I of England wore a red wig because her own red hair was falling out, so all the rich men and women copied her and either dyed their hair red or wore red wigs. In France, King Louis XIV, who was also going bald, started the fashion of *elaborate*

中国和日本，染发被视为一种非传统行为，在年轻人中，高达百分之六十八的女性和百分之二十的男性用头发的颜色来反映他们的个性。

假发是一个很时髦的词，它也是财富和地位的象征。古埃及人为了清洁，剃头后戴上假发。一个人的社会地位越高，他戴的假发就越大，埃及艳后就有许多不同款式、不同颜色的假发，另一个埃及女皇在重要场合戴的假发很沉，必须在别人的帮助下才能行走。英国女王伊丽莎白一世由于自己的红发褪色就佩戴红色的假发，于是，全英国有钱人都把头发染成红色或戴红色的假发。法国路易十四头发快要秃顶时，便开始佩戴精致的

---

individuality *n.* 个性
occasion *n.* 时机；场合

wig *n.* 假发
elaborate *adj.* 精心制作的

wigs. Naturally, everyone wanted to look like him, so they all started to wear wigs, too. At one time, forty wig makers were employed full-time just to make wigs for the people in the palace of Versailles!

These elaborate wig fashions went over to England, which always copied the French for style. Wigs became common for the middle and upper classes in England and France. They were powdered white because people thought this *flattered* the face and made their eyes look brighter. The fashion spread to divisions of the law, the army, and the navy, each of which had its own style of wig. However, by the end of the 1700s, hairstyles for women became *extravagant* to the point of *ridicule*. Rich women would spend hours with hairdressers who built tall wire cages on the women's heads. They covered the cages with hair and wigs and then *greased* the hair with fat so the white powder would stick to it. Finally, they decorated the hair with jewels, feathers, ornaments, and even flowers with

---

假发。自然，每个人都模仿他开始戴假发。有段时间，凡尔赛宫专门雇了四十个专业人士为他们做假发。

英国人经常效仿法国，所以这种精致的假发很快就传到英国。在英国和法国，假发在中上层人们中也开始流行起来。他们都开始在假发上抹白色粉末，他们认为这样能使脸更有光泽，眼睛也更有神。这股潮流渐渐传到法律部门、陆军和海军，这些部门各自都有自己独特的假发款式。但到18世纪末，妇女的发型变得很夸张，几乎到了荒唐的地步。富有的女性会花上几个小时让理发师在头发上做一个很高的，用金属丝制成的笼子，然后用头发和假发覆盖笼子，再在头发上抹上油脂，这样就能吸附住白色粉末，最后再用珠宝、羽毛、鲜花来点缀头发，这些鲜花还配有水箱来保持

---

flatter *v.* 奉承；使（某人）显得好看

ridicule *n.* 嘲笑

extravagant *adj.* 过度的；奢侈的

grease *v.* 在……上涂油

water containers to keep them fresh. The women would wear their hair this way for two or three weeks. Obviously, they had to sleep in a sitting *position* at night and they could not wash their hair, but once a week they had to "open the hair" to get rid of the insects living in it. Fortunately, the French revolution in 1789 put an end to such extravagance, and hairstyles became simple again.

In the twentieth century, women in western cultures used their hair to show their growing independence. They often *simplified* their hairstyles to fit their busy lifestyles. For example, in the 1920s and 1930s, women cut their hair as a symbol of *liberation*. In the 1950s and 1960s, many women in the United States used wigs to save time. Instead of styling their hair every morning, they would wear a pre-styled wig. Some women *alternated* between several wigs so that they could choose a style or color to match their clothes or even their mood!

它们的新鲜。妇女们的这种发型会持续两到三周。当然，她们晚上睡觉时只能坐着，也不能洗头，但她们每周会把头发打开驱除里面的虫子。幸运的是，1789年的法国革命终止了这种奢华的行为，人们的发型又变得简单了。

在20世纪，西方国家的妇女用发型来展示她们日趋独立的个性。她们通常用简单的发型来适应她们繁忙的生活。比如，在二三十年代，她们用剪头表示她们的解放。五六十年代，许多美国妇女佩戴假发来节省时间。她们佩戴事先设计好发型的假发，这样就不用每天早晨都去设计发型了。有的妇女会交替使用不同的款式或颜色来搭配不同的衣服甚至是心情。

---

position n. 位置
liberation n. 解放

simplify v. 简化
alternate v. 交替；轮流

Due to such changes, fashionable hairstyles no longer became limited to the rich—they were for everyone. And as the popularity of movies and television grew, women started to copy the hairstyles of famous stars, such as the short cut of Greta Garbo or the *platinum blond* hair color of Jean Harlow. More recently, thousands of American women *imitated* Jennifer Aniston's "*Rachel*" haircut seen on the popular TV show *Friends*. Men and boys also copy the hairstyles of movie or sports stars. In England, for example, boys often have their hair cut like the British soccer player David Beckham.

Today's hairstyles have become more relaxed and *individual*, so both men and women can choose a style that fits their life and expresses their personality. Whether they are rich or poor, people can choose the color or style of their hair—or even of a wig—to suit their own taste.

由于这种变化，时髦的发型不再是有钱人的专利了，每个人都可以拥有。随着电影电视的普及，妇女们开始效仿明星的发型，如葛丽泰·嘉宝的平头或珍·哈露的银灰色金发。最近，几千名美国妇女们又开始模仿受欢迎的电视剧《老友记》中瑞切尔的扮演者珍妮佛·安妮斯的发型。男人或男孩们喜欢模仿电影或体育明星的发型。比如，在英国，男孩们就经常模仿足球运动员贝克汉姆的发型。

当今的发型已变得很随便，很个性化，因此，大家都选择一种适合自己生活且能展现自己个性的发型。人们不论贫富，都会选择符合自己品位的头发，甚至假发的颜色和发型。

---

platinum blond （头发的）银色   imitate v. 模仿；仿效

individual adj. 个体的

22

Where Did Certain Wedding Customs Come From?

Everywhere around the world, weddings are celebrated with some kind of *ceremony*. These ceremonies differ between cultures, but many of the customs *associated* with wedding ceremonies—such as the wedding ring, the wedding dress, the wedding cake, and throwing *confetti*—come from common beliefs and similar ancient

一些婚俗的起源

世界各地的婚礼都有一定的仪式来庆祝，不同的文化有不同的庆祝方式，但婚礼上相关的习俗，如婚戒、礼服、结婚蛋糕和扔糖果都源于共同的信仰和相似的古老传统。

---

ceremony *n.* 仪式
confetti *n.* 糖果

associate *v.* 相关；发生联系

traditions.

The idea of the wedding ring started with the ancient Hindus. It was not considered to be a symbol of love in the beginning. It was, in fact, a sign that a *down payment* had been given for the woman and that she was no longer available. In some tribes in Africa, women are still bought. In 1964, a chief of the Maasai tribe offered 150 cows, 20 goats, and $750 cash to buy American actress Carroll Baker. This was a lot, considering the best Maasai fighter then paid $200 and 12 cows for a wife!

The ancient Greeks and Romans took the idea of wedding rings from the Hindus, and they also kept the ring as a sign that a young lady was "sold." Christian societies *adopted* the ring around the year 1000 as a sign of *fidelity*. The ring, a circle with no beginning and no end, also was a symbol of eternity. The Scandinavians did not adopt

---

结婚戒指是古印度人发明的。最初，他们并不认为戒指是爱情的象征。事实上，它是付给妇女的首期付款，这样这个妇女就不能再嫁给别人了。在非洲的一些部落，妇女仍然可以买卖。1964年，马塞部落首领用150头牛，20头羊和750美元的现金购买美国电影明星卡罗尔·贝克，这笔彩金非常丰厚。部落最英勇的战斗能手花200美元和12头牛就可买到一个妻子。

古希腊和罗马人从印度人那里借鉴了结婚戒指的习俗，他们也把戒指当作"买"到新娘的凭证。大约公元1000年左右，基督教徒把戒指看作是忠诚的象征。没有开始也没有结尾的圆环——戒指也成了永恒的象征。

---

down payment （分期付款中的）头期款；预付订金   adopt v. 收养
fidelity n. 忠诚；忠实

the custom of wedding rings until the late 1600s. Before then, they preferred to break a gold or silver coin and have each partner keep one-half.

There are also various beliefs about which hand and finger to put the ring on. The ancient Greeks and Romans wore the ring on the fourth finger of the left hand because they believed that a *vein* ran directly to the heart from that finger. However, wedding rings are not worn on the left hand in every country. In Chile and Germany, couples exchange rings when they get engaged, wear their rings on their left hand until they are married, and then *switch* them to their right hands. In Russia, there is no special finger for a wedding ring. However, people there usually wear a ring on the right hand to indicate they have a partner. In some countries, like Brazil, couples wear rings on the left hand and have their names *inscribed* inside

---

直到17世纪后期，斯堪的纳维亚才开始在婚礼时使用戒指。在此之前，他们喜欢把一块黄金或银币平分，一人保留一半。

关于戒指应该戴在哪只手，哪根手指上也有很多不同的说法。古希腊和罗马人把戒指戴在左手的无名指上，因为他们认为血管直接从心脏通到这个手指。但是现在很多国家的人都不会把戒指戴在左手。在智利和德国，订婚时双方交换戒指，在他们正式举行婚礼前都把戒指戴在左手，婚礼之后就会把戒指移到右手。在俄罗斯没有特别规定哪只手戴戒指。但是人们通常把戒指戴在右手上来表示他们已经有另一半了。在有些国家，如巴西，夫妇左手戴戒指，他们把名字刻在戒指里：新郎的刻着新娘的名

---

vein *n.* 血管；静脉

inscribe *v.* 题写；刻

switch *v.* 转移

the ring: the bride has the groom's name in her ring and vice versa. In Sweden, women wear three rings: one for *engagement*, one for marriage, and one for motherhood.

Today many brides marry in a white dress, which symbolizes purity. This tradition started in the 1500s. Before that time, brides wore their best dress, and the color did not matter. Today, in the United States and Britain, brides wear white dresses and follow the tradition of wearing, "something old, something new, something borrowed, something blue." Each "something" has a special meaning. "Something old" is a symbol of past happiness and symbolizes the transfer of these feelings to the bride's marriage. "Something new" symbolizes the hoped-for success of the marriage, and it often takes the form of a new dress. "Something borrowed" represents the hope that the *loyalty* of friends will continue through

---

字，新娘的刻着新郎的名字。在瑞典，妇女们戴三枚戒指：订婚时一枚，结婚时一枚，生孩子时一枚。

当今许多新娘在婚礼时穿白色服装以象征纯洁，这个传统始于16世纪。在此之前，新娘都穿上她们最漂亮的衣服，对颜色倒无可挑剔。现在，在美国和英国，新娘穿上洁白的服装并遵循古老的着装传统：有旧的、新的、借来的，还有蓝色的。每项都有特殊的意义："旧的"指的是过去的幸福，他们希望把这种幸福延续到新娘的婚姻中；"新的"指的是希望婚姻成功，通常是穿一套白色的服装；"借来的"指的是朋友间的忠诚能延续到婚姻中；"蓝色的"指的是忠贞，因为蓝色本身就象征着忠

---

engagement *n.* 订婚   loyalty *n.* 忠诚

the marriage, and "something blue" *stands for* fidelity, since blue is the color that symbolizes this value. In Japan, white was always the color for a bride even before it became popular in Western cultures. A Japanese bride may sometimes change her dress two or three times on her wedding day. She may start with a traditional kimono and end with a Western-style white dress. In Finland, brides wear white dresses and golden *crowns*. After the wedding ceremony, guests cover the bride's eyes, and the unmarried women dance around her as she puts the crown on one of their heads. Whoever she crowns, it is believed, will be the next bride.

White is not the color worn by brides everywhere. In China and Pakistan, brides wear red, which symbolizes happiness. In Samoa, brides wear a dress made of material from the bark of a tree, along with fresh flowers and a crown of mother of pearl. In the past, it was

---

贞。白色是新娘的颜色。这种思想在西方流行之前就已经在日本存在了。婚礼那天，新娘一般要更换两三次衣服，最开始是传统的和服，最后是西式的白色套裙。在芬兰，新娘穿白色套裙，戴黄金做的皇冠。婚礼结束后，客人就蒙上新娘的眼睛，未婚少女就围着她跳舞。她取下皇冠戴在谁的头上，谁就会是下一位新娘。

并非所有的新娘都穿白色婚服，在中国和巴基斯坦，红色象征幸福。在萨摩亚，新娘穿用树皮做的衣服，配上鲜花和珍珠皇冠。过去，新娘和

---

stand for 代表

crown *n.* 皇冠

common practice in many cultures for the bride and the bridesmaids to wear the same color as a way of confusing evil spirits that might hurt the bride. Today, this tradition is still present in the Philippines.

The idea of the wedding cake is common throughout the world. Originally, the wedding cake was not eaten by the bride. It was thrown at her! People thought that throwing cake at a bride would bring her *fertility*. It originally started with throwing wheat, which later took the form of little cakes. Later, the cakes were piled on top of each other, and a higher pile meant more *prosperity* for the couple. Finally, a French chef thought of the multi-layered cake that is common in Western cultures today. Many countries have their own *traditional* cakes: the Irish have a fruitcake, in the Ukraine it is a wedding bread, in Denmark it is an *almond* cake with beautifully decorated sugar work, and in France they have caramel-coated

---

伴娘通常穿同一种颜色的衣服来迷惑邪恶的灵魂，避免新娘受到伤害。现在菲律宾仍然保留着这种传统。

全世界的人几乎都会在婚礼时分享结婚蛋糕。最初蛋糕不是给新娘吃的，是扔给她的。因为人们认为向新娘扔蛋糕才会使她繁衍后代。最初是扔小麦后来改扔小蛋糕。最后把蛋糕一块块地堆在一起，堆得越高表明夫妇俩今后的日子越兴旺。终于有个法国的厨师想到了如今在西方非常普遍的多层蛋糕。许多国家都有自己的传统蛋糕：爱尔兰是水果蛋糕，乌克兰是结婚面包，丹麦是杏仁蛋糕，上面还有甜品装饰，在法国是由焦糖做的

---

fertility *n.* 可繁殖性

traditional *adj.* 传统的

prosperity *n.* 繁荣；成功

almond *n.* 杏仁

cream puffs.

Throwing things at the couple to wish them fertility or prosperity is also common throughout different cultures. People in the United States traditionally threw rice at couples as they left the place where they got married. When people learned that the rice was making birds sick, they began throwing *birdseed*. Unfortunately, the seeds injured some brides and grooms. Therefore, Americans today often blow bubbles or throw confetti, which is a mix of small pieces of colored paper, often in the form of hearts, horseshoes, and slippers. (The word confetti comes from an Italian word meaning "sweetmeats", which are mixed nuts, dried fruit, and honeyed almonds.)

Of course, there are variations to this tradition: Italians throw sugared almonds to *symbolize* the sweet (sugar) and bitter parts

---

奶油泡芙。

　　向新婚夫妇扔东西来祝福他们能够繁衍后代和兴旺发达的方式在全世界都很普遍。美国人传统上在离开婚礼举行地时会向新婚夫妇扔大米。当人们发现大米能使小鸟生病时，就改扔鸟食。不幸的是，有时这些鸟食使新娘和新郎受伤，因此当今美国人都改吹泡泡或扔喜糖，这些喜糖包括有颜色的小纸片，呈心状、马蹄状或拖鞋状。（单词confetti来自于意大利，意思是"甜肉"，包括坚果，干果，蜂蜜杏仁。）

　　当然，这种传统也有别的说法：意大利人向新婚夫妇扔甜杏仁，象征生活的甜蜜和痛楚，而捷克人则扔豌豆，罗马尼亚人扔糖果和坚果。曾经

---

birdseed *n.* 鸟饵；鸟食

symbolize *v.* 象征

of life; in the Czech Republic, people throw peas; in Romania, it's sweets and nuts. Throwing shoes once was preferred over throwing wheat, rice, or birdseed, because in the old days people believed shoes were a symbol of fertility. The Inuit of North America still have this tradition. It is also common today in the United States and Britain to tie shoes to the back of the newlyweds' car.

Even in our modern traditions, we still use *ancient* symbols to show our wishes for marriage unions to be happy and fruitful. Most of these wedding customs from around the world have things in common and come from shared human values. Though many customs are based on ancient traditions and *superstitions* that we may not be aware of today, they have the same purpose: They all celebrate marriage and wish the new couple well.

有段时间，扔鞋比扔小麦、大米或鸟食更受人们的欢迎。因为在过去，人们认为鞋是繁衍后代的象征。北美的因纽特人仍保留这一传统，今天美国人和英国人举行婚礼时都会把鞋系在婚车后面。

即使在现代，我们仍沿用一些古老的象征来表达对新婚夫妇的祝福，希望他们幸福、美满。这些新婚传统大都是相似的，都有全球共同的价值观作为支撑。尽管许多习俗都来自古老的传统和今天我们无法理解的迷信，但都有一个共同的目的：都为婚礼祝福并希望新婚夫妇生活幸福美满。

---

ancient *adj.* 古老的   superstition *n.* 迷信

Who Are the Cyber Angels?

You are on the Internet checking your e-mail. There is a *file* attached to one of the messages, so you open it. After that, you start *having problems with* your computer. It starts very slowly, or it won't start at all. The names of your computer files start changing. Then you start getting calls from your friends—

何谓网络天使？

当你正在上网查收邮件时，有个文件夹附在某条信息后面，你打开后，发现电脑被病毒感染了。最初病毒侵入非常慢，几乎察觉不到。电脑的文件夹开始更名，你朋友的电话也接踵而至，他们收到你

---

file *n.* 文件夹　　　　　　　　have problems with　在……（方面）有问题

they are receiving e-mails from you that you never sent. Your computer probably received a *virus* through the e-mail attachment. Viruses are unsafe programs that *sneak* into and sometimes ruin computers. Some viruses can even find private information on your computer and deliver it to dishonest people. Now there is an organization that protects people from viruses and other types of Internet crime: It is called Cyber Angels.

Cyber Angels is part of Guardian Angels, a *volunteer* organization that makes the world safer for us to live in. But Guardian Angels didn't originally protect people from Internet crimes. It began before most people even had computers. The organization started in 1979 with Curtis Sliwa. At the time, Sliwa was the night manager at a McDonald's in a dangerous part of New York City. With his workers, he started the "Rock Brigade". The Brigade started to improve

---

的邮件，可这些邮件你从来都没发过。通过黏附的那个文件夹，电脑病毒侵入了你的计算机。病毒是危险的程序，它可以侵入甚至破坏你的电脑。有的病毒还能找到你电脑上的个人隐私然后把这些信息传给不可靠的人。现在成立了一个叫"网络天使"的组织使人们免受病毒和其他网络罪犯的侵害。

守护天使是一个志愿者组织，以确保人们居住社会的安全为目标，网络天使是它的一个组成部分。守护天使最初不是防范网络罪犯的，在大多数人拥有电脑之前它就已经存在了。它是1979年由科特恩·斯里瓦创办的。那时，斯里瓦是纽约一个危险地带的麦当劳夜班经理，他和员工一起

---

virus *n.* 病毒　　　　　　　　　　　　sneak *v.* 偷偷摸摸地做
volunteer *n.* 志愿者；志愿兵

the *deteriorated* neighborhood by planting trees, cleaning up *vacant* lots, sweeping the sidewalks, and in general making the area more beautiful. The Rock Brigade got awards from the community and government groups.

The neighborhood was cleaned up, but the streets were not safer. At that time in New York, crime had increased, but the city had no money to *hire* police to control the crime. Older people would come to McDonald's because Sliwa would walk them home safely. One day, a retired transit worker begged him to do something about the street *muggers*. At this point, Sliwa decided to expand his clean-up program to include patrolling the subway. From his workers, he put together a multiracial group of volunteers. In the beginning, there were twelve volunteers, and together with Sliwa they were known as the "Magnificent Thirteen". Without weapons, they would walk the

---

成立了"石头组织"，这个组织采取很多措施改善周边恶劣的环境，比如植树，清扫空地和人行道。总之，使这个地区变得非常漂亮。这些做法受到了社区和政府的嘉奖。

周边环境改善了，可街道并没有因此而更加安全。那时的纽约，犯罪率急剧提高，政府没有钱雇用警察来控制犯罪。老人都愿意去麦当劳，因为斯里瓦会把他们安全地送回家。有一天，一位退了休的临时工人请求他采取措施制止街头行凶者。趁这次机会，他决定把清洁计划扩大到地铁。他从员工中挑选出不同种族的人组成志愿者，最初只有12人，加上他本

---

deteriorate *v.* （使）恶化
hire *v.* 雇用

vacant *adj.* 空着的
mugger *n.* 行凶抢劫者

streets and ride the subway in the most dangerous areas to find the gang members who had been robbing people. Then they would hold these criminals until the police came to arrest them. They gradually took back the neighborhood; it was no longer *infested* with crime.

Since then, Guardian Angels have *patrolled* areas such as subways, shopping mall parking lots, concerts, public parks, and streets that are dangerous. As the streets are getting safer, the Guardian Angels are spending more time on safety education and programs for children in poor areas. They also have programs to help and *escort* senior citizens and people with disabilities so these people can *participate* in activities without fear. They have speakers who go out to schools and other organizations to talk about self-defense. Today, the Guardian Angels even include professional teachers and counselors for young people after school.

人，被称为"了不起的13人"。他们徒手在街道和地铁中巡查，在最危险的地方寻找那些曾抢劫过的黑帮团伙。如果抓到了，就押着这些人，等警察来逮捕。渐渐地，周边恢复了宁静，那个地方也再没被罪犯所困扰。

从那时起，守护天使一直在地铁、商场、停车场、音乐厅、公园和危险的街道上巡逻。随着街道越来越安全，守护天使就把时间花在对贫苦地区孩子的安全教育上。他们还发起了帮助和陪伴老人和残疾人的活动，使这些人能够勇敢地参与到这些活动中。他们还有一些演说家去学校和其他组织讲解自卫方面的知识。现在，他们还有专业老师和辅导员对青年进行课余辅导。

---

infest *v.* 骚扰
escort *v.* 护送

patrol *v.* 巡逻
participate *v.* 参与

The Guardian Angels have become famous for making people feel safe in their neighborhoods. Nearly twenty years after this organization began, a woman asked Curtis Sliwa how he planned to make people feel safe online. Sliwa thought about that question, and he decided to start another program for a new problem: Internet crime. Cyber Angels, Sliwa's program for online safety, started in 1995 and is the oldest and largest cyber-safety program. It's an information and help line for those who come across trouble through the Internet, or those who want to make sure they never do. It combats Internet crime like viruses, *fraud*, and online behavior that threatens people or hurts children. By working with law *enforcement* agencies, the group has been instrumental in catching criminals associated with the Internet. Cyber Angels also provide classes on Internet issues for parents, teachers, librarians, and the general

---

守护天使因使周围环境日益安全而闻名。在他们成立组织20年后，有个妇女询问科特恩·斯里瓦怎样能使网络变安全。考虑了一阵后，他决定为解决网络犯罪发起新的行动，斯里瓦为保护网络安全而发起的"网络天使"活动始于1995年，是最早最大的网络安全程序，对那些遇到网络问题或想要确保自己不遇网络问题的人来说，它就是信息检索站和帮助热线。它与病毒、诈骗和网络恐吓、伤害少儿的网络犯罪做斗争。他们和执法部门一道致力于网络罪犯的抓捕工作。网络天使还就网络问题为家长、

---

fraud *n.* 欺骗；骗子   enforcement *n.* 实施；强制

public so they can take advantage of the vast resources of the Internet in safety.

Anyone, male or female, can become a Cyber Angel or Guardian Angel, but these organizations have other special requirements for their volunteers. Cyber Angels must be at least eighteen years old, and they must pass a background check. The group especially needs the services of skilled workers such as law enforcement workers, teachers, computer experts, and people in the *legal* field. Not everyone who wants to be a Cyber Angel is accepted. Guardian Angels also have high *expectations* of their volunteers. They must be at least sixteen years old, have no serious criminal record, and be going to school, working, or able to prove how they support themselves otherwise. After the organization looks at an applicant's background, he or she must complete a training program that lasts

---

老师、图书管理员和大众提供讲座，以便他们能安全利用网络资源。

无论男女，任何人都可以成为网络天使和守护天使的一员，但这两个组织也对志愿者提出了要求。网络天使至少要年满18岁，除此以外，还得对其背景进行全面审查。这些组织尤其需要有经验的工作者，如执法员、教师、电脑高手和懂法的人。并不是每个想成为网络天使的人都能如愿以偿。守护天使对职员的要求也很高，必须年满16周岁，没有严重的犯罪前科。他们要么读书，要么工作或用其他方式来证明能独立养活自己。申请者在接受背景考察后，必须参加一周10个小时，为期3个月的培训。培

---

legal *adj.* 合法的 　　　　　　　　　　　　expectation *n.* 期待；预期

ten hours a week for three months. There is training in self-defense, first aid, the legal code, how to make a citizen's arrest, and how to patrol. It is not necessary to be a martial arts expert to become a Guardian Angel. Attitude and *dedication* are more important than anything else. However, it helps if you know how to defend yourself. Once they are trained, members have to make two patrols a week, which totals about eight hours. The Guardian Angels do not carry weapons. Before they go out on patrol, each member is searched for weapons and drugs just to make sure. If they are found to have any of these, they are immediately dismissed.

As nonprofit organizations, Guardian Angels and Cyber Angels do not receive money from the government or big *corporations*. Angels do not get a salary; they are all voluntary workers. The organization gets some money from individual contributions to help

---

训内容包括自卫、急救、法律常识、如何抓捕人以及怎样巡逻，但这并不说明守护天使的成员必须精通武术，处世的态度和奉献精神比其他什么都重要。如果你知道应如何保护自己将会对你的工作有更大的益处。他们一旦接受训练，每周都得参加两次巡逻，共8个小时。守护天使并不携带武器。在巡逻前，每个成员都得搜身看是否携带武器或毒品以防万一。一旦发现携带了这些东西，他们将立即被开除。

作为一个非营利性组织，守护天使和网络天使没有政府的拨款或大企业的赞助，这些天使也没有工资，都是志愿者。这个组织接受个人捐助

---

dedication　*n.* 奉献；献身　　　　　　corporation　*n.* 公司；企业

in communities that need them. Today, the organization has 5,000 members in 67 cities in the United States, Canada, and Mexico. Popular support of Guardian Angels has grown in other parts of the world, too, and over twenty chapters or groups have been created around the world. The first Guardian Angel chapter outside the United States was started in London, and now there are *additional* European chapters in Nottingham, England, and Milan, Italy. In South America, there are Guardian Angels in Rio de Janeiro, Brazil, and we can also find them in several cities in Japan.

The Guardian Angels and Cyber Angels spread the idea of taking responsibility and becoming a power for good. Their actions have improved the lives of the people they serve—especially young people—as well as those of the volunteers themselves. For over twenty-five years, their idea has *inspired* young people. Now, it continues to do so as it spreads around the world.

来扶持那些需要帮助的社区。现在，这个组织遍布美国、加拿大、墨西哥的67个城市，已有5000多名成员。在世界其他国家也有，并新成立了近20个机构。在美国以外的第一个分部创建于伦敦，后来相继在诺丁汉、英国、米兰和意大利也成立了分部。在美洲南部、里约热内卢、巴西也有守护天使。日本的有些城市也能找到这种组织。

守护天使和网络天使将承担责任和成为正义的力量这种思想广泛传播，他们的行为改善了所服务群体的生活方式，尤其是青年人，也包括志愿者。在整整25年里，他们的这种思想鼓舞了许多年轻人。在传播思想的同时，他们的精神也继续鼓舞着更多的人。

---

additional *adj.* 附加的；额外的　　　　　　inspire *v.* 鼓舞

Why Is the Renaissance Important?

During the period of the Middle Ages (from about 500 C.E. to the mid-1400s) there were no great changes in the way of life in Europe. People did what their fathers did before them, and there were few new *inventions* or discoveries. Most people believed in what they were told and did not care about anything outside their lives. One reason

文艺复兴运动为何重要?

中世纪（从公元500年到15世纪中期）的欧洲，人们的生活方式没有太大变化，仍按照祖辈的方式生活着，很少有新的发现或发明。许多人坚信世代相传的东西，而对他们生活之外的一切事情都不在

---

invention *n.* 发明

for this may be because only a few people received an education, and books were scarce. Then, a change began. People became better educated, trade and industry developed, the arts *flourished*, and explorers discovered new lands. We call this great change the Renaissance, which in French means "rebirth". The Renaissance, which took place in Europe between the thirteenth and sixteenth centuries, was a new *stage* in the history of the world.

Some people think that the Renaissance got started when the Turks took over the Greek city Constantinople (now Istanbul) in 1453. Greek scholars left Constantinople and settled in other parts of Europe. In these new locations, they taught Greek and shared their *precious* books. The study of classical Greek and Roman writers and thinkers began again, and a new desire for learning spread throughout Europe.

People began to inquire into everything, and some began to question their beliefs and ways of thinking. In Germany, Martin Luther started a revolt against the *conventions* of the Roman Catholic

---

意。其中一个原因是因为只有少数人受过教育，书籍是非常稀少的。后来情况发生了变化，人们受教育的状况有所改善，贸易和工业迅速发展，艺术繁荣，许多探险家还发现了许多新大陆。这种巨大的变化被称作"文艺复兴"。在法语里是"重生"的意思。文艺复兴发生在13到16世纪的欧洲，是世界史的一个新开端。

有的人认为文艺复兴始于1453年土耳其人侵占希腊城君士坦丁堡（今伊斯坦布尔），希腊学者离开君士坦丁堡在欧洲其他地区定居。在这些新地区，他们教希腊语，与当地人共享珍贵的书籍。对古希腊和罗马作家与思想家的研究又重新恢复，新的学习热潮席卷整个欧洲。

人们开始对所有的事物进行探究。有人开始质疑他们的信仰和思维方

---

flourish *v.* 茂盛；繁茂
precious *adj.* 珍贵的

stage *n.* （发展的）进程，阶段或时期
convention *n.* 大会；惯例

Church. Soon, other Christians agreed that the Church needed to change, and several new Christian religions were established.

Other people began to think about new types of government that were based on the *democratic* values of ancient Greece. Italy, the birthplace of the *Renaissance*, was organized into city-states that governed themselves. Though wealthy families and the Church held much of the power in these areas, the city-states were moving a step in the direction of government by the people. The most famous political thinker of the Renaissance was Niccolo Machiavelli. In his book on government entitled *The Prince*, he stated that a good leader could do bad and dishonest things in order to preserve his power and protect his government. Though people in his own time thought that Machiavelli was evil for saying these things, his book is now famous and modern political thinkers respect some of his ideas.

The "new learning" taught people to think in new ways, and it

---

式。在德国，马丁·路德对罗马天主教的传统进行革新。不久，其他的基督教徒也认为教会需要改革，于是建立了几个新派基督教。

还有一些人开始考虑根据古希腊的民主价值观成立新的政府。文艺复兴的发源地——意大利组建了城邦，实行自治。尽管富人和教会在这些地区掌握了很大权力，城邦正在向由人民统治的政府方向演变。文艺复兴时期最著名的政治思想家是尼科洛·马基雅维利，他著有一部论述政府的书，书名为《王子》，书中讲述了一个优秀的领导人为了巩固政权和保住政府也可能做坏事或不诚实的事。尽管那时的人们认为他说的这些事看起来很邪恶，但他的书很受欢迎，当代政治思想家非常尊崇他的观点。

"新思想"教导人们用新的方式思考，还鼓励有天赋的人绘画、雕

---

democratic *adj.* 民主的   renaissance *n.* 文艺复兴

also encouraged gifted people to paint pictures, make statues and buildings, and write great literature. In fact, some of the best artists of the day did all of these things. As a result, when a person today is skilled in many areas, he or she is often called a "Renaissance man" or a "Renaissance woman".

The artistic developments of the Renaissance first happened in the Italian city of Florence, and then they spread to other Italian cities. As a result of trade and banking, cities like Florence, Venice, and Milan became very *wealthy*, and their rich citizens had both the time and money to enjoy music, art, and poetry. These cities produced great painters and *sculptors*, like Michelangelo, Leonardo da Vinci, and Raphael. These artists created some of history's finest works of art. For example, Michelangelo spent four years painting thousands of feet of curved ceiling in the Vatican's Sistine Chapel. To do this, he had to learn a whole new style of painting. He also

刻、建筑以及创作文学作品。事实上，那个时期优秀的艺术家都具备这些技能。因此，如果当今有人在很多领域精通，他（她）就会被称为"文艺复兴之男性"或"文艺复兴之女性"。

　　文艺复兴时期的艺术发展最早始于意大利的佛罗伦萨，接着传播到意大利的其他城市。由于贸易和银行业的兴起，佛罗伦萨、威尼斯、米兰都变得非常富裕，富裕的市民既有时间也有金钱去欣赏音乐、艺术和诗歌。这些城市也出现了大量的画家和雕塑家，如米开朗琪罗，列奥纳多·达·芬奇和拉菲尔。这些艺术家创作了一些历史上最优秀的艺术作品，例如，米开朗琪罗花了四年的时间为梵蒂冈的西斯庭圣母大教堂几千英尺的弧形

wealthy *adj.* 富有的　　　　　　　　　　　　sculptor *n.* 雕塑家

had to paint lying on his back beneath the ceiling as paint dripped down onto his face. Despite these *obstacles*, he created one of art's greatest masterpieces.

A new kind of architecture also began in the Renaissance. It *blended* the old, classical styles with new ideas. Again, it started in Florence. A cathedral there had been started in 1296, but it remained unfinished for over 100 years because no one could figure out how to build the curved roof that it needed. Then architect Filippo Brunelleschi invented a new type of dome that was higher and grander than any from the classical era. The dome marks the beginning of Renaissance architecture.

From Italy, interest in the arts and new ways of thinking spread to other countries. The Netherlands became famous for great painters; England produced many writers, including William Shakespeare; and Spain had the literature of Cervantes. The new *passion* for learning

---

屋顶绘画。为了完成这幅作品，他必须学会一种全新的画法。他还得在绘画时仰卧在天花板下面，绘画用的颜料滴落在他的脸上。尽管有这些障碍，他还是创造了世上最杰出的艺术作品之一。

文艺复兴时期还兴起了一种新式建筑。它把过去的古典风格与新的思想融为一体。这种建筑风格也是在佛罗伦萨兴起的。那里有一个大教堂，始建于1296年，但在接下来的100年间都未曾完工，因为没人知道该怎样修建它所需要的弧形屋顶。接着建筑家布鲁涅内斯基发明了一种新型圆屋顶，这种圆屋顶比古典时期任何一种都高大壮观。圆屋顶标志着文艺复兴建筑的开端。

从意大利开始，人们对艺术和新的思维方式的兴趣传播到了其他国家。荷兰因有伟大的画家而闻名，英国出了很多作家，包括莎士比亚。西

---

obstacle *n.* 障碍；障碍物

passion *n.* 激情；热情

blend *v.* 混合

also led to amazing discoveries in science by Galileo, Kepler, and Newton. Some of these findings went against the most basic beliefs of the time. For example, Galileo's discovery that the sun, not the Earth, was the center of the solar system got him into serious trouble with many *religious* people. They forced him to say that he had been wrong about his discovery, even though he knew he was right.

The development of the printing press in Germany by a man named Johannes Gutenberg helped more than anything to spread the new ideas of the Renaissance. Before that time, books were scarce and very expensive because they were written by hand. Gutenberg discovered how to use a moveable metal type, and his first book was published in 1455. Printing was a very important invention. With it, books were made more cheaply and quickly than ever. *In addition*, most books had been written in Latin before, as this was thought to be the language of study. However, with the

---

班牙拥有塞万提斯的文学作品。这种新的学习热情也带来了科学上惊人的发现，如伽利略、开普勒和牛顿的新发现，其中一些发现有悖于那个时期的绝大多数信仰。比如，伽利略发现太阳，而不是地球，才是太阳系的中心。这一发现使他与许多宗教人士发生了严重冲突。他们强迫他承认自己的发现是错误的，即便他知道自己是正确的。

德国的活版印刷是一个叫约翰内斯·谷登堡的人发明的，它比任何事物都更有效地推动了文艺复兴时期新思想的传播。在此之前，书籍很稀少而且很昂贵，因为都是手抄本。谷登堡发明了活版印刷，他的第一本书于1455年印刷。印刷是项非常重要的发明，有了它，书籍比以前更便宜而

---

religious *adj.* 宗教的   in addition 另外；而且

Renaissance, the middle classes could now afford books, and they wanted books in their own languages. They also wanted a greater variety of things to read, such as books on travel, poetry, and romance. Printing helped make the works of the best writers and all kinds of knowledge available to all.

About the time printing was discovered, sailors were *setting out* on voyages of discovery. Now that the Turks were masters of the eastern Mediterranean, it was no longer possible to trade with India by the old land route. A new way had to be found, perhaps by sailing around the coast of Africa—or perhaps by sailing around the world! There were many explorers around this time, including Columbus, Vasco de Gama, Cabot, Magellan, and Drake. Representing countries throughout Europe, these men sailed new waters and discovered new lands, including the Americas. With all this travel, tools for exploration and *navigation* improved, and better ships were

---

且数量也更多了。另外，以前大多数书籍都是拉丁语，因为当时拉丁语被认为是做学问所使用的语言。但是，随着文艺复兴的到来，中产阶级买得起书籍了，所以就希望能看到用自己的母语写成的书。他们还希望能读到各种题材的书，比如有关旅游、诗歌和浪漫故事等等。印刷使优秀作家的作品及各种知识能面向普通大众。

就在印刷术发明时，海员开始航海探险。因为土耳其人成了地中海东部的主人，再由原来的线路与印度人做生意已经不可能了。必须开辟一条新的航线，沿着非洲海岸或环球航行。这时期有很多伟大的探险家如哥伦布、瓦斯科·达·伽马、卡博特、麦哲伦、德鲁克等。他们代表着遍布欧洲的一些国家。这些人在新的水域中航行，发现了新大陆，这其中就包括

---

set out 出发；启程

navigation *n.* 航行；航海

made. As people traveled, they gained new ideas that helped to change their way of living. For example, Europeans now wanted goods—such as *spices*, silk, and gold—from far away countries.

The Renaissance didn't begin suddenly when Constantinople was taken over by the Turks or when the first book was printed in 1455. Forces that brought it about had been developing for many years as Europeans began to desire and gain new knowledge. From this new learning came the great changes that we call the Renaissance. These advancements—from the discovery of printing to a renewed interest in art and *literature* and the discovery of new lands—affected almost every area of European life. They also formed the basis for many parts of our modern life and beliefs. This is why some people think of the Renaissance as the beginning of modern history.

美洲。有了这些航行，探索的工具和航海技术得到了很大改善，船的质量也越来越好。人们在旅行时，汲取了新思想，从而改变了他们的生活方式。例如，欧洲人可以从遥远的国家得到诸如香料、丝绸和黄金等物品了。

文艺复兴并不是在土耳其侵占君士坦丁堡或1455年第一本书籍印刷出来后才突然兴起的。欧洲人的求知欲望愈来愈强，引起文艺复兴的力量已经蓄积了很多年。这种新的学习热潮给社会带来了巨大变化，这些变化就被称作"文艺复兴"。从印刷术的发明到人们对艺术和文学的再度感兴趣，再到新大陆的发现，这些进步几乎影响了整个欧洲的各行各业，成为我们现代生活方式和信仰的基础。这就是为什么有的人把文艺复兴看作现代史的开端。

---

spice *n.* 香料

literature *n.* 文学

What Is the Most Popular Sport in the World?

Soccer—which is called football in most places—is the world's most popular sport. It is played in parks, fields, schools, and streets all over the world. It has about 250 million male and female players in more than 200 countries, and it has even more fans. In fact, an *estimated* 33 billion people around the world watched the 2004 World Cup tournament, making it the world's most watched television sporting event—it even *surpasses* the Olympics.

世界上最受欢迎的体育运动

英式足球（在很多地方简称为足球）是世界上最受欢迎的体育运动项目。在全世界，不管是在公园、田野、学校还是在大街上都可以看到人们在踢足球。足球遍及二百多个国家，有二亿五千万左右的足球运动员（包括女性），还有比这还多的球迷。实际上，据统计，全世界有三百三十亿人观看了2004年的世界杯，使它成为全球收视率最高的体育项目，甚至超过了奥运会。

estimate *v.* 统计；估计　　　　　　　　　　surpass *v.* 超越；胜过

The exact origins of modern soccer are unknown. However, records show that the Chinese and Japanese played similar games over 2,000 years ago. Later, the ancient Greeks and Romans played it. The Romans took the game to Britain, which became the undisputed birthplace of modern soccer.

In Britain, the game came to be called football, because only the players' feet could touch the ball. However, when the British played football, it was more like war than a game. Towns and villages played against each other, and sometimes up to 500 people played on each team. There were even annual contests where large groups ran wildly from village to village playing the game. One game could last all day. Naturally, many people died and were injured. Several kings banned the game, passing laws against the sport because it was so rough and because soldiers preferred to play it than to *concentrate* on *military* training. Even Queen Elizabeth I had players in

现代足球的确切起源我们无从得知。但是，有记录显示在两千多年前中国和日本就有类似的运动。后来，古希腊人和古罗马人开始踢足球。罗马人把这项运动带到英国，英国就无可争议地成为现代足球的发源地。

在英国，这种运动被称为足球，因为球员只能用脚接触球。但是，英国人踢球更像一场战争而不是比赛。小镇的人和村庄的人对抗。有时一个球队就有五百人。每年还会有年终总决赛，各队阵容强大。他们挨个村庄踢球，一场比赛能踢一整天，自然就会有许多人死亡或受伤。于是，有几个国王下令停止这种运动，还颁布法律来禁止，因为这种运动太粗鲁，还因为士兵都跑去踢足球而不注意军事训练了。女王伊丽莎白一世甚至把

concentrate *v.* 集中　　　　　　　　　　　military *adj.* 军事的

London put into jail because they caused so much damage to shops and public *property* when they played in the streets. But the game was too popular to be stopped.

Football was played in many English schools as early as the 1800s, but it had no formal rules. Later, two sets of rules were developed. One set was *devised* at a school called Rugby, where players could handle and run with the ball. The game of rugby developed from these rules. Other schools preferred the "hands-free" game. In 1848, the general rules of the hands-free game were established at Cambridge University.

The Football Association of England was formed in 1863. At that time, university students created slang by adding -er to words they shortened. The name soccer developed from adding -er to the letters S, O, and C (from the word Association). However, the game is still known as football in most parts of the world besides North

---

伦敦的球员送进监狱，因为他们在大街上踢球时毁坏了许多店面和公共财产。但这种运动太受人们欢迎，以至于政府根本禁止不了其盛行。

早在19世纪许多英国学校就兴起了这项运动，但缺乏明确的规则。后来形成了两套规则。第一套是由一个叫橄榄球的学校设计的，根据这套规定，球员可以握着球跑。橄榄球就是由此而产生的。其他学校更倾向于"把手空出来"，用脚踢球。1848年，人们在剑桥大学制定了关于足球运动的大体规则。

英国足协成立于1863年，那时，大学生在他们简化的词后加"er"变成俚语，足球名称"soccer"来源于S，O，C后加"er"（即来自单词association）。但是，除北美外，其他许多地方仍把它称为football。而

---

property *n.* 财产；所有权　　　　　　　　　　devise *v.* 设计

America, where soccer is more commonly used. Football quickly became popular throughout Europe and South America, and in 1900 it became one of the first team sports played in the Olympic Games. In 1904, seven nations—Belgium, Spain, Sweden, France, the Netherlands, Denmark, and Switzerland—met in Paris to form FIFA, the Federation Internationale de Football Association. FIFA has been the governing body of the sport ever since. Today, it has 204 member countries. Every four years, the world's strongest national football teams compete to be world *champions* and to get the World Cup—a golden *trophy*. The World Cup started in 1930. Beginning in 1958, it was held alternately in Europe and the Americas, but since 1996 it has been held in Asian countries as well.

Traditionally, football had been a game for male players, but now it has become popular with female players. Though women played football in China about 2,000 years ago, this was not heard of again

---

在北美，用soccer的更为普遍。足球迅速在欧洲和南美洲盛行起来。到了1900年，足球成为奥运会的第一批团体项目之一。1904年，有7个国家——比利时、西班牙、瑞典、法国、荷兰、丹麦和瑞士在巴黎共同成立了国际足联(FIFA)。从那时起，国际足联就成为这项运动的领导机构，现今有204个成员国。每隔4年，世界上最强的球队竞争世界冠军，获得黄金奖杯——世界杯。世界杯赛始于1930年。从1958年起，交替在欧美国家举行，但自1996年起，亚洲国家也开始举办。

传统上足球是男人的运动，但现如今，女性也开始踢足球了。尽管在2000年前，中国的妇女就开始踢足球，但直到20世纪20年代这种运动才

---

champion *n* 冠军　　　　　　　　　　trophy *n* 奖品；奖杯

until the game reappeared in the country's school *curriculum* for girls in the 1920s. Appropriately, the first Women's World Cup was held in China in 1991.

Throughout history, football was considered "unsuitable for women" in Europe, and they were banned from playing it. However, in the 1970s women were allowed to play again, and the sport's popularity started to grow. Certainly, this *trend* will continue. Since 1996, women's football has been included in the Olympic Games, and today more than 7 million young girls play in the United States alone. The United States is a newcomer to the women's game, but has won the World Cup twice and has also won two Olympic gold medals and one silver medal. Other new nations for women's football include Brazil, Nigeria, and Japan. The players of the American team were the first women players to be paid as full-time professionals, but now other countries are following their lead. Though salaries are over

---

再现于中国学校的体育课程里，女孩才再次投身其中。准确地说，第一届女子世界杯赛是1991年在中国举行的。

从历史上看，足球在欧洲被称为一种"女性不宜"的运动，女性被禁止踢足球。然而，到了20世纪70年代，女性又允许参与了，这项运动便也随之开始流行，而且还将继续流行下去。从1996年起，女子足球被列入奥运会项目。现在仅在美国就有七百万年轻女孩踢足球。美国虽然后来才有女足，但它已赢得过两次世界杯赛，还赢过奥运会两金一银。另外几个后来拥有女足的国家是巴西、尼日利亚和日本。美国队的球员是最先作为职业球员领取薪金的，但现在许多国家都竞相仿效。然而最好的女足球

---

curriculum *n.* 课程

trend *n.* 倾向

$100,000 a year for the top female professionals, they are nowhere near the average of $5 million that their male *counterparts* make.

Every country thinks it has the best football team, but they all admit that Brazil is the world's greatest football-playing country. The sport was first introduced to Brazil by a British man named Charles Miller, who started a team there. In 1899, this team played the country's first recorded game of football. Today, football is a way of life in Brazil. The Brazilian team was the first team to win the World Cup five times, and it has more professional teams than any other country in the world. Its talented players, such as Pele, Garrincha, Zico, and many others, have made Brazil famous throughout the world. These players started out very poor and became *incredibly* wealthy. They became true idols. Their *influence* can be seen on the young boys in the streets of poor neighborhoods throughout Brazil.

员一年只可获得十万美金，这个数目远远不及男性球员的薪金，他们平均每年可获得五百万美金。

　　每个国家都认为自己的球队是最棒的，但他们都承认巴西队是世界上最好的球队。足球最初是由一位名叫查尔斯·米勒的英国人引入巴西的。他在巴西组建了一支球队。1899年，这支球队踢了该国有记载的第一场足球。当今，踢球已成为巴西人的一种生活方式。巴西队是第一支赢得世界杯五连冠的球队，巴西也是世上职业球队最多的国家，其出色的球员如贝利、加丁查、济科等使巴西足球闻名全球。这些球员最初都非常贫困，现在却极为富有，已经成为人们心中真正的偶像。其影响可以从贫苦社区大街上的孩子

---

counterpart *n.* 职位（或作用）相当的人　　　　incredibly *adv.* 非常
influence *n.* 影响

The dream of nearly every young boy growing up in poverty there is to become a professional football player one day. It seems to be their only way of *escape from* poverty, and thus this sport has a greater influence on their lives than almost anything else.

Brazil is not the only country with football stars. Britain's David Beckham has become an idol for many young people. They read magazines about him and wait for his latest hairstyle to copy. In Tokyo, a giant three-meter (nearly ten-foot) statue of Beckham made entirely of chocolate was made to promote a new kind of chocolate. Advertisers use him to sell many things, and of course he makes millions of dollars from each advertising *contract*.

Football is the one of the oldest sports in the world. It has been gaining fans across the globe for over 2,000 years, and it doesn't show any signs of stopping. Will football continue to be the most popular sport in the world? Most people think it will!

身上看到。贫困中的孩子都梦想将来有一天成为职业球员，这似乎成了他们脱离贫困的唯一途径，因此这项运动的影响对他们来说胜过一切。

巴西并不是唯一拥有球星的国家。英国的贝克汉姆已成了许多年轻人的偶像。这些年轻人阅读杂志上有关他的报道，模仿他最新的发型。在东京，有尊完全用巧克力做的三米高的贝克汉姆的塑像是专门用来推销一种新型巧克力的。他也成了许多产品的代言人，当然他也从这些产品合同中获利丰厚。

足球是世界上最古老的运动之一。两千年来，它赢得了全球众多的球迷，而且没有停止的迹象。足球还将继续成为全世界最受欢迎的运动吗？绝大多数人认为答案是肯定的。

---

escape from 逃脱；摆脱   contract *n.* 合同

26

How Did Convicts Help Settle Australia?

The British were not the first Europeans to arrive in Australia. Dutch, Spanish, and Portuguese explorers had passed through the vast continent before them without giving it much notice. When an Englishman, Dampier, did land in what is today New South Wales, he *condemned* the land as barren and useless. Then the British explorer Captain James Cook proved his *predecessor* wrong. He landed at Botany Bay in New South

罪犯在建立澳大利亚中的作用

英国人并不是第一批到达澳大利亚的欧洲人，荷兰、西班牙和葡萄牙的探险家曾经穿越眼前这片广阔的大陆，但却没有在意。当一个英国人丹皮尔在今天的新南威尔士登陆后，他认为这块土地贫瘠，没有实用价值。接着英国探险家詹姆士·库克证明了先辈的错误，他于

condemn *v.* 谴责   predecessor *n.* 前辈；前任

Wales in 1770, and with his botanist, Joseph Banks, he proved that the eastern shores were rich and *fertile*. Although Captain Cook gave an excellent report on all the land he had seen in Australia, the British government made no effort to form a *settlement* there for several years.

For many years it was the policy of the British government to send men and women found guilty of breaking the law to America. There, as punishment, these prisoners were forced to work on big farms until they had served out their sentences, and they were then set free. This policy of sending criminals abroad was called "transportation".

However, all this changed with the loss of the American colonies. In 1776, the American colonies declared their independence from Britain. When they became the United States of America, no more *convicts* could be sent there. The British government was in a difficult position. People were still being sentenced to transportation, but

---

1770年登陆新南威尔士的伯特尼湾，和植物学家约瑟夫·班克斯一起证明了东海岸的富饶与多产。尽管库克船长把他在澳洲的所见所闻写成了精彩的报道，但英国政府在之后几年内并没有向澳洲移民的打算。

许多年来，英国政府制定了一项政策把犯了法的公民发配到美洲。作为惩罚，这些囚犯必须在大农场劳作直到刑满为止，然后才将他们释放。这种把囚犯遣送出国的政策叫"流放"。

但是，这种情况随着美洲殖民地的独立而改变。1776年，美国殖民地正式宣告脱离英联邦的统治。当美利坚合众国成立后，囚犯就不能再被遣送去美洲。这样英国政府就陷入两难的境地，因为囚犯仍要被流放但却

---

fertile *adj.* 富饶的；肥沃的
convict *n.* 囚犯

settlement *n.* 移民

there was nowhere to send them. Soon, the jails were overcrowded.

Joseph Banks, Captain Cook's botanist, suggested New South Wales as a good place for a convict settlement. "The soil is good there," he said, "and soon they will grow all their own food." Lord Sydney—after whom the city of Australia is named—had the task of looking after the British colonies. He decided to try Banks' plan. He selected Captain Arthur Phillip, a naval officer, to take charge of the new settlement.

In May 1787, the First Fleet, consisting of eleven ships, left England for New South Wales. *On board* were about 1,400 people, of whom 780 were convicts. The rest were mainly soldiers to *guard* the convicts and seamen to work on the ships. About 20 percent of the convicts were women; the oldest convict was eighty-two, and the youngest one was about ten years old. The voyage to Australia was very slow. It took eight months; six of these were spent at sea,

---

没有地方可去，而英国的监狱已经人满为患。

詹姆士·库克的植物学家约瑟夫·班克斯向政府建议，新南威尔士是流放囚犯的理想之地。他说那里的土壤很肥沃，不久那些囚犯就能自食其力。悉尼爵士负责看管英国的殖民地，澳大利亚城市悉尼就是以他的名字命名的。他决定执行班克斯的计划，任命亚瑟·菲利普船长为海军军官，负责这些新的殖民地。

1787年5月，由11艘船只组成的"第一舰队"离开英国驶向新南威尔士。船上共有1400人，其中780人是囚犯，剩下的主要是看管囚犯的士兵。其中20%的囚犯是妇女，年纪最大的已经82岁，年纪最小的只有10岁。去澳洲的航行特别慢，要花8个月的时间，其中6个月都要在海上度

---

on board 到船上；在船上   guard v. 看守；监视

and two were spent in ports to get supplies. The fleet finally arrived in Botany Bay in 1788. Two more convict fleets arrived in 1790 and 1791, and ships continued to come to other ports in Australia for over seventy years.

A major problem of the convict system was the severity of its *punishments*. Among the convicts on the First Fleet was a woman who was transported for stealing a coat. The British also transported a man who had received a sentence of fourteen years for killing a rabbit on his master's property. Others were transported only because they supported different political opinions. There were many real criminals who were transported as well, but by today's standards many of the convicts would not be considered criminals.

Conditions on the ships were *deplorable*. Ship owners were paid "per head," or for each person they transported. To make as much money as possible, the owners overcrowded the ships. The convicts

---

过，剩下的两个月在各码头补充储备物品。这支船队最终于1788年到达伯特尼湾，后来又有两只囚犯船队分别于1790，1791年到达。接下来在长达70多年的时间里，又有一些船只陆续到达澳洲的其他港口。

囚犯制度最大的问题就是刑法的严厉性。"第一船队"的囚犯中有一名妇女仅仅因为偷了一件上衣。英国政府还流放了一个因杀了主人家的兔子而被判入狱14年的男子。其他被流放者多是因为他们坚持不同的政治信仰。这些被流放者中也有真正的罪犯，但依照今天的标准来看，他们根本就称不上罪犯。

船上的条件极差，由于船主按人头收费，为了挣更多的钱，轮船经常处于爆满状态。囚犯被铁链锁在甲板下，那里既没有阳光也没有新鲜空

---

punishment *n.* 惩罚 deplorable *adj.* 糟透的

were chained below deck, where there was no sunlight or fresh air. They suffered a lot, and many died on the way. Because so many died on the ships, later the government paid a bonus to ship owners whose passengers had arrived safe and sound at the end of the journey.

For convicts who made it to Australia, conditions were a little better. Those who were well behaved were *assigned* to settlers as workers or servants, and if they worked for good people, they served out their *sentences* under pleasant conditions. Other convicts worked in groups for the government. They did various kinds of jobs, such as clearing land, making roads and bridges, and constructing public buildings. Those convicts who refused to work or tried to escape were severely punished.

Convicts could win their freedom back more quickly with good behavior. They could qualify for a "Ticket of Leave" or a "Certificate

气。他们经受了很多磨难，很多人在中途死去。由于船上死亡人数太多，政府给那些把囚犯安全、健康送达目的地的船主一笔奖金。

对那些到达澳洲的人来说，那里的条件会稍微好一点。那些表现好的人都派给当地定居者当工人或仆人，如果能为好人服务，他们就会在良好的条件下服完刑期。其他的囚犯则分成小组来为政府服务，做着各种各样的工作，如清理土地、修路建桥和修建公共建筑。那些不愿工作或试图逃跑的人则会受到严厉的惩罚。

如果囚犯表现得好，他们很快就能重获自由。他们就有资格得到"休假票"或"自由证书"。获得自由的囚犯可以在这个国家里自由流动，并

assign *v.* 指派；分配   sentence *n.* 判决；宣判

of Freedom." Convicts who got their freedom were allowed to move around the country and work in any kind of profession they liked. Soon, many educated ex-convicts became lawyers, teachers, and business owners. Others bought land and became rich settlers.

Convicts were not the only settlers in the country; free settlers had been coming from Britain and starting farms since 1793. In the beginning, the convicts were a great help to the new settlers. But later, when the number of free settlers grew, they *objected to* the transportation of convicts. They thought it was unfair that their new land was filled with *criminals*. By 1840, objection was so strong that no more convicts were *transported* to the mainland. Instead, they were sent from there to Tasmania, an island south of Australia.

Convicts had never been sent to western Australia, but in the middle of the nineteenth century, the colony there suddenly asked for them. There was a shortage of labor in the region, and the colony

---

从事他所喜欢的任何职业。不久，许多受过教育的前囚犯成了律师、教师、商人等。其他人则购买土地，成了富有的殖民者。

囚犯并非这个国家唯一的殖民者。自1793年以来，自由殖民者就从英国来到这里经营农场。最初，囚犯对这些人来说非常重要，但随着自由殖民者人数的扩大，他们反对流放囚犯，认为如果新的土地上到处都是囚犯是很不公平的。到了1840年，这种呼声越来越高，囚犯不再被流放，他们被遣送到澳洲南部一个叫塔斯马尼亚的小岛上。

囚犯从未被送到澳洲的西部，但是到了19世纪中期，那里的殖民地开始需要囚犯。这个地区缺乏劳动力，而殖民地又只有靠囚犯的劳作才能

---

object to 反对

transport *v.* 运输

criminal *n.* 罪犯

could only progress with convict labor. Britain supplied the colony with convicts starting in 1850 and ending in 1868, and the convicts helped build it up by constructing roads, bridges, and public buildings.

A total of 162,000 men and women — transported on 806 ships — came as convicts to Australia. By the time the British policy of transportation ended, the population of Australia had *increased* to over a million. Without the convicts' hard work, first as *servants* and later as settlers, it wouldn't have been possible for the government and the free settlers to create a nation. The transportation of convicts is an *essential* part of Australia's history. Today, many Australians acknowledge their convict ancestors and are grateful for their contributions to the country.

发展下去。从1850年到1868年这段时期，英国就一直向这一殖民地提供囚犯，帮助修路建桥和一些公共建筑。

共有806只船运送了162,000名囚犯到达澳洲。在英国流放政策结束前，澳洲的人口已达到一百万还多。如果没有那些先当仆人后做殖民者的囚犯的辛勤劳动，政府和自由殖民者也就不可能创造出一个国家。囚犯的流放是澳洲历史上不可或缺的一部分。当今，许多澳大利亚人都承认他们的囚犯祖先，并对他们为这个国家所做的贡献心存感激。

---

increase *v.* 增加

essential *adj.* 基本的；必要的

servant *n.* 仆人；佣人

27

How Do Greetings Differ Around the World?

There is a range of different *greetings* around the world, from a simple "hello," a handshake, a kiss, or a bow, to sticking out your tongue in Tibet! But how you shake someone's hand in one country may differ from the custom in another. In some countries you kiss as a greeting, but how many times do you kiss? Which *cheek* do you start with? In which countries do you bow? Here are

世界各地不同的问候语

从一句简单的"你好"、一个握手、一个亲吻或是一个鞠躬到西藏的伸出舌头以示问候，世界各地有一系列不同的问候方式。但是在一个国家里，如何问候也许会随着他国的风俗而有所不同。在一些国家，亲吻作为一种问候，但要亲吻多少次呢？要从哪一侧脸颊开始亲吻呢？在哪

---

greeting *n.* 问候；招呼

cheek *n.* 脸颊；面颊

some examples of greetings from a few parts of the world.

A bow or a light handshake with eyes averted is the usual greeting in most Asian cultures where people do not like to have body *contact* when greeting. In China and Taiwan, shaking hands is customary, but people often nod their heads or give a slight bow as well. The Chinese like to *applaud*, and a visitor may be greeted with a group of people clapping their hands. When you are applauded, you must return the applause or say thank you.

In Japan, a *graceful* bow is the traditional greeting. The Japanese have also adopted the Western handshake, but the handshake is light, with eyes averted. When being introduced, visitors can make a slight bow to show respect for Japanese customs. In Korea, as in Japan, the bow is the traditional form of greeting. For men, a handshake sometimes follows the bow. Women do not shake hands with men; they usually just nod.

些国家你要拥抱呢？接下来列举世界上几个地区表示问候的例子。

　　一个带有目光交流的鞠躬或轻轻地握手，在大多数具有亚洲文化背景的国家是正常的问候方式。在那里，人们打招呼时不喜欢有身体上的接触。在中国和台湾，握手是习俗，但人们也经常点头示意或微微鞠个躬。中国人喜欢鼓掌以示欢迎，遇有来访者，就会有一些人拍手鼓掌表示欢迎。当你受到欢迎时，你也必须鼓掌或说声谢谢以示回敬。

　　在日本，优雅的鞠躬是一种传统的问候方式。日本人也采纳了西方的握手方式，但握手只是轻轻地并带有目光交流。当被介绍时，拜访者可以做一个轻轻地鞠躬以示对日本风俗的尊敬。在韩国，像日本一样，鞠躬同样是一种传统的问候方式。对于男性，先鞠躬后握手，妇女则不与男性握手，她们通常只是点头而已。

---

contact　*n.* 接触；联系　　　　　　　　　applaud　*v.* 拍手喝彩；称赞
graceful　*adj.* 优雅的

People in the Philippines are much more touch-oriented than those in other Asian cultures. Here, handshaking is a common custom, with both men and women shaking hands in a friendly fashion. Filipinos may also greet each other with a quick flick of the eyebrows.

In Malaysia, people greet each other saying, "Where are you going?" But this is not really a question. The polite answer is, "Just for a walk." In India, people greet each other with "Namaste". As they say this, they bend or nod and put their *palms* together as though they are praying.

European greetings vary from shaking hands to kissing. In Britain, people do not like physical contact very much, so they *opt* for the handshake. Between friends they just say, "Hi!" or "How are you?" However, you *are* not *supposed to* say how you really are. Between close friends and family, kissing is normal. Germany follows the same rules as Britain. In France, however, kissing is the rule. Multiple

---

生活在菲律宾的人比其他亚洲国家的人更倾向于东方化握手，这是再普通不过的了，在男女中广泛流行。菲律宾人也可能快速动一下眼眉以示问候对方。

在马来西亚，人们打招呼时会说："你去哪里？"但这并不是在真的提问。礼貌的回答是"散散步"。在印度，人们打招呼时说"namaste"。当他们说这个词时，他们弯腰或点头并双手合十，就好像在做祈祷一样。

欧洲的问候方式会从握手过渡到亲吻。在英国，人们非常不喜欢身体上的接触，所以选择握手这一方式。在朋友中间他们就说"嗨"或"你好啊？"然而，你一定别真问"你好吗？"在亲密的朋友间和家人中，亲吻是正常的事。德国遵循着与英国一样的问候方式，而在法国，亲吻则是一

---

palm *n.* 手掌

be supposed to 应当；应该

opt *v.* 选择

kisses are normal and will vary from region to region. In most places, a two-kiss greeting is polite, but in Paris, the greeting is four kisses, starting with the left cheek. In Brittany, there is a three-kiss greeting, and in most other parts of France it is a two-kiss greeting. The exception is the south of France, where sometimes five kisses are not unusual. In the Netherlands, three kisses are expected, and you always start and finish kissing on the right cheek. If you're greeting a very close friend or an older person, four or five kisses are normal. In Spain, Austria, and Scandinavia, there is a two-kiss *ritual*. In Spain, you always begin with the right cheek. In Belgium, it's one kiss for a person about the same age as you, but three kisses to show respect for a person who is more than ten years older than you. Many may think that Italians would do a lot of kissing as a form of greeting, but the usual greeting there is a *handshake*. For friends, handshakes and hugs are the norm. Kissing is restricted to very close friends and

---

种习惯。多数亲吻是正常的问候，并将随着区域的不同而变化。在大多数地区，亲两下是礼貌的，但是在巴黎，则要亲四下，从左脸开始。在布列塔尼，要亲三下。在法国大多数地方都是亲两下，但法国南部除外，在那里有时亲五下都是常见的。在荷兰，被亲三下是受尊重的表现，要从右脸开始和结束。如果你问候的是一位非常亲密的朋友或一位长者，亲四五下都是正常的。在西班牙、奥地利、斯堪的纳维亚，有亲两下的礼仪。在西班牙，你总是要从左脸开始。在比利时，对于像你一样大的人要亲一下，但对于比你大十多岁的人亲三下以表示尊重。很多人会认为意大利人有亲很多下的礼仪。其实，最普遍的是握手，对于朋友而言，握手和拥抱则很正常。对于亲密的朋友和家人，亲吻是有一定限制的，但对于先从哪边脸

---

ritual *n.* 仪式；典礼   handshake *n.* 握手

family, and there are no special rules as to which cheek to kiss first.

Americans shake hands, using a firm grip. They are taught to do this to show honesty. They also look at someone in the eye when they greet them, to show they are not shy or weak. Americans also say, "Hi!" or "How are you doing?" As in Britain, they don't really expect you to answer that question. Hugs are used among close friends, though there are variations *depending on* where in the United States people live.

Handshakes are important in the Middle East and can be quite long. Most Arabs shake hands every time they meet someone and every time they leave. This *applies* wherever they meet—in the street, at home, or in the office. In Saudi Arabia, they shake hands on meeting, talk for a while, and then shake hands again. This can happen ten times a day with the same person. Arabs will kiss and hug friends of the same sex as a form of greeting, and they also look

---

颊开始则没有特殊规定。

美国人握手, 而且很用力, 他们这样做以示诚恳。当他们问候某人时也会用眼睛看着对方, 以示他们既不害羞又不软弱。美国人常说"嗨"或"最近怎么样啊?"和英国人一样, 他们并不是真的希望你会给予回答。亲密的朋友中常常使用拥抱, 但是这也随着美国人居住地方的不同而有所变化。

在中东, 握手是非常重要的问候方式, 而且要握很久。大多数阿拉伯人每一次见面和分别都要握手。无论他们在哪相见——街上、家或办公室, 这种习俗都很适用。在沙特阿拉伯, 他们一见面就握手, 谈一会儿, 然后再握手, 这样一天中就可能与同一个人握十次手。阿拉伯人将亲吻和

---

depend on 取决于……   apply *v.* 适用

the person in the eye.

Greetings in Senegal take the form of handshakes, and they are even more significant there. In Senegal, a person will stop doing something really important to spend ten minutes greeting a person that he or she has seen an hour ago. This is to *acknowledge* the existence of another human being and is seen as a *priority* in Senegalese culture. Every member of the community greets every other member, regardless of status or wealth. They must greet each other even if one of them is in the middle of a business *transaction* or is discussing something with someone else. In the greeting, they repeat the other person's family name over and over to acknowledge that person's entire family, both living and dead. The Senegalese are *offended* if you do not greet them first before asking a simple question. For example, if you ask, "Where did he go?" without offering a greeting first, you may get a response such as, "He went

---

拥抱作为欢迎同性朋友的方式，并会用眼睛看着对方。

塞内加尔采用握手这一问候方式，而且这一方式在那里非常重要。在塞内加尔，一个人会停下手中正做的十分重要的事，花十分钟向别人打招呼，而这个人可能是一个小时前刚见过的。这表明对对方存在的承认，并在其文化中被视为一种优待。无论地位和财富如何，这个社会中的每一个人都会和其他人打招呼。即便其中一个人正在处理业务或正和其他人讨论事情，他们也必须彼此问候。在问候中，他们不断重复着另一个人的姓，来承认其整个家庭成员，包括活着的和已故的，如果在问他问题前，不和他先打个招呼，塞内加尔人就会觉得被冒犯了。比如说，如果你问："他去哪里了？"在事先没打招呼的前提下，你很可能会得到这样的回复，

---

acknowledge *v.* 承认
transaction *n.* 交易；办理

priority *n.* 优先；优先权
offend *v.* 冒犯；得罪

to learn how to greet." This is another way of saying that you are rude.

There are many variations in South American countries, but the general rule is a handshake at first meeting and a kiss on the cheek between close friends. Men often *embrace* if they know each other well. Strangers do not *address* each other by their first names when they are being introduced. Their title (Mr., Mrs.), followed by their first name, is a common greeting, because it indicates friendship and respect. Eye contact is essential in South America.

Some cultures have variations on these common greetings. For example, the Inuit of North America traditionally used the kunik in place of the kiss. The kunik involves placing noses next to each other and lightly rubbing or *sniffing*. Most Inuit now use their lips to kiss, but the kunik is sometimes still used with children. Though most New Zealanders use a handshake when greeting, the tradition

---

"他去学如何问候了。"这是暗示你很粗鲁的另一种表达方式。

在一些南美国家有许多不同的问候方式，但最普遍的方式是在熟悉的朋友间一见面就握手并在脸颊上亲一下，如果很熟了，则拥抱一下。陌生人之间被介绍时，不直呼双方的名字，而是在名前加上"先生"或"夫人"的头衔，这是很普遍的，表明友谊和尊重。眼睛的交流在南美也同样重要。

文化背景不同，问候方式也不同。例如，北美的因纽特人，传统上用亲鼻代替亲吻，有时两个人的鼻子轻轻地摩擦或抽搐一下鼻子。现在大多数因纽特人亲吻，但是传统的问候方式有时仍在孩子之间使用。虽然

---

embrace *v.* 拥抱
sniff *v.* 用力吸；闻到

address *v.* 用（某姓名或头衔）称呼某人

of the native Maori people is to press noses together to show trust and *closeness*.

In many Asian countries, people like to exchange business cards when they first meet, but they have special customs for doing this. To show respect for the other person, they use both hands when giving and taking a card, and they take time to study the other person's card before putting it away. They also never write on someone else's card.

Of course, these are only a few of the greetings used around the world. There are even more variations in other countries. Learning about these customs not only makes us more polite travelers, but also gives us *insight* into the differences between people around the world, as well as an understanding of each country's special values.

大多数新西兰人打招呼时握手，但当地毛利人的传统方式则是一起挤压鼻子以示信任和亲密。

在许多亚洲国家，第一次见面时人们喜欢互换名片，这样做是有特殊讲究的。为了表明对另一个人的尊重，给或接名片时，要用双手收起来，仔细看对方的名片，从不在他人的名片上写字。

当然，以上列举的这些仅仅是世界各地问候方式中的少数几种。在其他一些国家，还会有更多不同的问候方式，了解这些风俗不仅能使我们成为礼貌的旅游者，也会让我们深刻地了解世界各民族不同的风俗，并了解每个国家各自的价值观。

---

closeness *n.* 亲密

insight *n.* 洞察力；洞悉

Who Is Maria Montessori?

In 1882, 12-year-old Maria Montessori had a very serious illness. She turned to her mother and said, "Do not worry, Mother, I cannot die; I have too much to do." Even at a young age, Maria believed she had a *purpose* in life. She had already decided she wanted to be an engineer. Most women in nineteenth-century Italy wanted to be wives and mothers.

玛丽亚·蒙特梭利是谁?

1882年,12岁的玛丽亚·蒙特梭利得了一场重病。她对妈妈说: "不要为我担心,妈妈,我不会死的,还有好多事情等着我去做呢。"这样小的年纪,玛丽亚就坚信她的生活是有意义的。她下了决心要做一名工程师。19世纪的意大利,大多数妇女想的是如何做贤妻良母。但

purpose *n.* 重要意义

But Maria was not an ordinary girl. She was highly intelligent and extremely determined. She never worked as an engineer. But she did become the first woman in Italy to become a doctor. Then she used her understanding of science and medicine to develop the Montessori method of teaching. By the time she was 40 years old, she was world famous.

Maria Montessori was born in 1870 in the Ancona region of Italy. Her father was an engineer and builder. He was very traditional and believed that women should be wives and mothers. Her mother came from a well-educated wealthy family. She believed that women had the right to be educated like men. Clearly, Maria took after her mother.

When Maria was 12, she told her parents she wanted to attend a *technical* school to prepare her for a career in engineering. She did very well in *mathematics* and science, which are important subjects for engineers. But her parents urged her to become a teacher

---

玛丽亚可不是一般的女孩儿。她非常聪明而且意志坚定。她没有成为工程师，但是，她成了意大利的第一位女医生，后来，她利用自己对科学和医学知识的理解，提出了儿童教育的蒙特梭利方法。40岁时，她已经名扬世界了。

玛丽亚·蒙特梭利于1870年出生在意大利的安科纳地区。她的父亲是位建筑工程师，为人非常传统，认为女人只要做好妻子和母亲就行了。而玛丽亚的母亲出身富庶，受过良好教育，她认为女人和男人一样有受教育的权利。显然，玛丽亚继承了母亲的观点。

12岁时，玛丽亚告诉父母她想上一所工业学校，为她将来做工程师作准备。她的数学和理科学得很好，而这些课程对工程师这一行很重要。

---

technical *adj.* 工业的；技术的　　　　　　　　mathematics *n.* 数学

instead because it was one of the few respectable *careers* for young women. Maria refused. "Never!" she said. "Anything but teaching!" Finally, Maria's father agreed to allow her to enter technical school. She was the only female student in the school.

Maria completed her technical studies, and then shocked her parents once more. She told them she didn't want to be an engineer after all. She wanted to be a doctor. Her father was even more upset this time. But Maria was determined to follow her dreams. She applied to the medical school at the University of Rome, but the director told her it was "unthinkable" for a woman to do such a thing. Maria then asked for help from the most powerful man in Rome, Pope Leo XIII. In 1893, Maria became the first female medical student in Italy. It was a very exciting, but difficult time.

The students in Maria's class *tormented* her with their mean

---

但是她的父母希望她成为一名教师，因为在当时，教师是年轻女性从事的极少数受人尊敬的职业之一。玛丽亚拒绝了，"决不！"她说，"我无论如何不做教师。"没办法，她的父亲只好同意她上那所工业学校。她是那里唯一的女生。

完成工业学校的学业后，玛丽亚再一次让父母吃了一惊。她说她不想当工程师了，她想当医生。这次她父亲被她搞得更加心烦意乱。但是，玛丽亚决定追寻自己的梦想。她向罗马大学医学院提出申请，但是院长告诉她，女人当医生根本就"不可想象"。于是，玛丽亚求助于罗马当时最有权力的教皇利奥十三世。1893年，玛丽亚成为意大利医学专业的第一名女生。随后是一段令人难忘又很难熬的日子。

玛丽亚班上的学生们对她恶语相加，想让她上不了课。那个时代，人

---

career *n.* 事业   torment *v.* 折磨；使痛苦

remarks. Her classes were almost *unbearable*. In those days, it was completely unacceptable for men and women to see a naked body together, even though it was for school. So Maria was forced to study the human body by examining dead bodies alone at night. Her mother helped her study for her exams because the other students refused to study with her. Even her father wouldn't speak to her or help in any way. Everyone tried to make Maria miserable so she would drop out of school. Maria had a lot of *willpower* and she wouldn't give up.

During her last year at school, Maria gave a lecture to the medical *faculty*. Many people came to hear her, but most came to laugh at her. Maria's speech was so amazing that the audience was *stunned*. Everybody applauded and cheered—even Maria's father, who didn't want to go to the lecture. Maria graduated in July 1896 and made

---

们绝不能接受男人和女人同看赤裸的人体，哪怕是为了学知识。所以，玛丽亚被迫在夜里独自通过研究尸体来学习人体知识。她的母亲陪她学习、准备考试，因为别的学生都不愿意和她在一起。她的父亲甚至不跟她讲话，更不肯帮一帮她。每个人都想迫使她停止学医。可是，玛丽亚意志坚强，她绝不放弃。

在医学院学习的最后一年，玛丽亚给医学院的全体教员做了一次讲座。许多人到场，但大多数是准备来嘲笑她的。然而玛丽亚的讲座非常精彩，征服了所有听众。大家热烈鼓掌欢呼，包括她的父亲，而他原本是不想来的。1896年，玛丽亚从医学院毕业，成为意大利有史以来的第一位

---

unbearable *adj.* 难以忍受的
faculty *n.* 全体教员

willpower *n.* 意志力
stun *v.* 使震惊

history as the first female doctor in Italy.

Maria Montessori practiced medicine in Rome for the next 10 years. However, she didn't make a lot of money because she often treated poor patients without charging them any money. She supported herself by lecturing at the University of Rome. In 1897, she worked in a psychiatric *clinic*. She wasn't paid for this work either. Montessori toured the city's mental hospitals and became interested in the treatment of mentally *retarded* children. She was very disturbed by their living conditions. She went from one hospital to another and studied the children for hours. Eventually, she decided that the children could learn if they were just given the chance. She began to write articles and give lectures about her studies.

In 1901, Montessori became the director of a school for the education of mentally retarded children in Rome. Most people

---

女医生。

后来的10年当中，玛丽亚·蒙特梭利在罗马从医。但是，她没有挣多少钱，因为她总是免费为穷人看病。玛丽亚靠在罗马大学教书养活自己。1897年，她在一家精神病诊所工作，这份工作也是没有报酬的。她到罗马的各个精神病院巡访，开始对治疗弱智儿童产生兴趣。她为他们的生活条件而感到不安。玛丽亚一家医院、一家医院地巡访，长达数个小时地观察、研究那些孩子们。最后她得出结论，只要给他们学习的机会，他们就能学会。于是，她开始写文章，宣讲自己的研究结果。

1901年，蒙特梭利到罗马的一个弱智儿童学校任校长。多数人认为

---

clinic *n.* 诊所　　　　　　　　　　　retarded *adj.* 身体或精神发育迟缓的

thought these children were hopeless. They were locked in rooms and treated like animals. The people who worked there threw food at them and kept them in rooms with nothing to touch or see or play with. Montessori believed that the children behaved like animals because they were treated that way. The first thing she did was to change their *environment* and their treatment. She gave them activities to do and things to play with. After a while, the children *responded*. They learned to read and write. They did things that no one believed they could ever do. Montessori's students did so well that they passed the national examinations given to other children their age. She was praised highly for her work. She was called a "*miracle* worker." Hundreds of newspaper and journal articles were written about her and her work with mentally retarded children. Montessori lectured about her findings and people everywhere

---

这些孩子已经不可救药。人们把弱智儿童锁在屋子里，像对待动物一样。学校的工作人员把食物朝孩子们身上扔，把他们关起来，不给他们任何可以触摸、观看和玩耍的东西。蒙特梭利则认为，孩子们之所以表现得像动物，是因为人们把他们当作动物来看待。她做的第一件事就是改变孩子们的环境和人们对他们的态度。她发给孩子们玩具，带他们开展活动。很快，孩子们就开始做出回应了。他们学会了读和写。他们甚至做到了别人都不相信他们能做的事情。蒙特梭利的学生们还通过了相同年龄正常孩子参加的国家考试。人们对她的工作给予了高度评价，称她是"创造奇迹的人"。数百篇报纸和杂志上的文章报道了她在智障儿童教育工作方面的事

---

environment *n.* 环境
miracle *n.* 奇迹

respond *v.* 回答；做出反应

wanted to learn her successful technique.

Maria Montessori's career was very promising at this time. She had fame and success, and she was excited about her future. She was also in love with her *assistant*, Dr. Guiseppi Montesano. When Maria discovered she was pregnant, she was forced to quit her job as director of the school. Unfortunately, Dr. Montesano didn't want to marry her. If anyone discovered that Maria had a baby and wasn't married, her career would be ruined. She went to the country to have her baby. Later she gave the baby to a family and visited him secretly. Nobody knew about her son until after her death.

Over the next several years, Montessori studied many subjects, including *psychology* and education, at the University of Rome. In 1907, she became director of the first Children's House school in a poor area of Rome called San Lorenzo. The school had

迹。蒙特梭利向人们介绍自己的方法，各地的人们都想学习她的成功之道。

这一时期，正是玛丽亚·蒙特梭利大有可为的阶段。她功成名就，憧憬着未来。正在这时，她坠入爱河，爱上了自己的助手吉塞皮·蒙泰萨诺博士。蒙特梭利发现自己怀孕了，只好辞去校长之职。可是，蒙泰萨诺博士并不想和她结婚。如果别人发现她未婚先孕，她的前程就毁了。她到乡下把孩子生下来，送给了一个人家，想孩子了，只能偷偷地去探望。直到她去世，人们才发现她还有个孩子。

在以后的几年中，蒙特梭利在罗马大学研修了许多科目，其中包括心理学和教育学。1907年，她到罗马一个叫作圣洛伦佐贫穷地区的第一所

assistant *n.* 助手　　　　　　　　　　　　　psychology *n.* 心理学

over 50 students from three to six years of age in a single room. People believed that these wild children could not be educated or controlled. Again, Montessori gave the children work to do, things to play with, and the freedom to learn on their own. She allowed them to make mistakes and to learn from them. The results were amazing.

Soon her students could read, write, and count—even the four-year-old! Visitors from around the world came to learn Montessori's teaching methods. She became famous everywhere. Within two years, all the *kindergartens* in Switzerland changed to the Montessori system. In 1909, she published a book called *The Montessori Method*. She continued her work by studying the needs of older children and developed teaching methods for them *as well*.

儿童福利学校担任校长。这所学校把五十多个三至六岁的孩子们关在一间屋子里。人们认为她管不了也教不好这些野孩子。这一次，蒙特梭利仍然给他们玩具，让他们做事，让他们有自己学习的自由。允许他们犯错误，并从错误中学习。她又一次取得了惊人的成绩。

很快，她的学生就学会了读书、写字和数数——就连四岁的孩子都行！世界各地的参观者们都来学习蒙特梭利的教学方法，她的名字家喻户晓。两年里，瑞士所有的幼儿园都改用蒙特梭利教学模式。1909年，她出版了《蒙特梭利教学法》一书。她继续研究大龄儿童的需要，研究适合他们的教学方法。

---

kindergarten *n.* 幼儿园　　　　　　　　　　as well 也；同样地

The success of the Children's House led to the opening of many other Montessori schools throughout the United States and Europe. The schools were for all children, not only those with learning problems. Alexander Graham Bell formed an American Montessori Society. Queen Victoria invited Montessori to London to honor the beginning of the use of the Montessori method in England. In Italy, Queen Mother Margherita supported the Roman Montessori Society. For nearly 50 years, Montessori lectured at training centers around the world. She wrote several books and never stopped working. She died in Holland at the age of 82. Her *determination*, independence, and hard work changed the world of education forever.

儿童福利学校的成功使整个美国和欧洲国家争相效仿，开办起采用蒙特梭利教学模式的学校。这些学校面向所有的儿童，而不仅仅针对那些有学习困难的孩子。亚历山大·格雷厄姆·贝尔成立了美国蒙特梭利协会。维多利亚女王邀请蒙特梭利到伦敦为英国蒙特梭利教学法活动的首讲仪式剪彩。在意大利，玛格丽塔女王资助罗马的蒙特梭利协会。将近五十年的时间里，蒙特梭利在世界各地的教学法培训中心讲课。她笔耕不辍，写了好几本书。82岁那年，她在荷兰去世。她的坚定决心、独立思考和勤奋工作给教育界带来了永久而深刻的变化。

determination *n.* 决心

Who Is J.K. Rowling?

J.K. Rowling is the *author* of the *Harry Potter* books. J.K.'s name is Joanne Kathleen. She was born in 1965 in a small town near Bristol, England. Joanne lived with her parents and her sister. The Rowling family was not rich. Joanne did not go to *special* schools. She was a quiet child. She loved to read and write stories. Joanne went to Exeter University, and she finished in 1987. She worked in different offices.

谁是J. K. 罗琳?

罗琳是《哈利·波特》一书的作者，她的全名是乔安·凯瑟琳·罗琳，1965年出生于英国布里斯托尔港附近的一个小镇上。她和父母、妹妹生活在一起，由于家境并不富裕，所以没去专业学校念书。她是个很文静的孩子，非常喜欢读书和写故事。后来，她被艾克赛特大学录取并于1987年毕业。她从事过不同的工作，利用空闲时间，她写了很

author *n.* 作家；作者   special *adj.* 特殊的；专门的

In her free time, she wrote more stories.

In 1990, Joanne's mother died. Joanne was sad, and she wanted to leave England. She saw a job in the newspaper for an English teacher. The job was in Portugal. She had an *interview*, and she got the job. In Portugal, Joanne married a Portuguese man. The next year, Joanne had a daughter, but she was not happy in her marriage. She left Portugal with her daughter and went to live in Edinburgh, Scotland, near her sister.

Life was very difficult for Joanne. She *took care of* her daughter. She was alone, and nobody helped her. She had no money and no job. She lived in a small apartment and began to write stories again. Joanne first thought about the Harry Potter story many years ago on a train. Joanne liked to go to a coffee shop to write. She sat there for many hours. She drank coffee and wrote. Her daughter slept beside her.

After five years, Joanne finished writing the first *Harry Potter*

多故事。

1990年，罗琳的父母去世，这让她非常伤心，决定离开英国。有一天，她在报上看到葡萄牙有个地方招聘英语教师，面试后她得到了这份工作。后来，她嫁给了一位葡萄牙人。并在第二年有了一个女儿，可她总觉得自己的婚姻不幸福。不久，她带着女儿离开了葡萄牙，回到了苏格兰的爱丁堡市，那里离她妹妹家很近。

罗琳的生活非常艰苦，孤身一人，还要照顾女儿，没有人帮助。此时她既没钱也没工作，住在一个很小的公寓里，重新开始了写作。在一次火车旅行中，她开始构思哈利·波特的故事。她喜欢在咖啡店里创作，一坐就是几个小时，一边喝咖啡一边写作，女儿就在她旁边睡觉。

五年后，罗琳完成了《哈利·波特》第一本书的创作。她把这本书拿

---

interview *n.* 面试；面谈   take care of 照顾

book. She sent it to many book *publishers*. They all said that they didn't like it. Finally, a publisher liked it, but the publisher said, "This is a children's book. Adults won't read it. You won't make a lot of money." In 1997, *Harry Potter and the Sorcerer's Stone* was in the bookstores. J.K. Rowling was very happy. Her dream to publish her book *came true*. The book was famous all over the world.

Now *Harry Potter* is in forty-two languages. The publisher was wrong about one thing: Everyone loves Harry Potter—children and adults. Over 100 million books were sold in 1999. Then two *Harry Potter* books became movies. J.K. Rowling wrote three more *Harry Potter* books after that. People all over the world want more *Harry Potter*. And what is J.K. Rowling doing now? She is writing another book!

给很多出版商看，但他们都不喜欢这本书。最后终于有一位出版商同意给她出版发行，但对她说："这是一本儿童读物，成年人是不会读的，你肯定赚不了多少钱。"1997年，《哈利·波特与魔法石》面世了，罗琳非常高兴，她作家的梦终于实现了，而且这本书一下就风靡了全球。

现在，《哈利·波特》被译成了42种文字，出版商的预计出现了错误，每个人都很喜欢哈利·波特——无论是孩子还是成人。1999年，销量达到10亿册，接着有两本《哈利·波特》被拍成电影，此后她又写了三本《哈利·波特》续集，全世界的人都期待更多的《哈利·波特》问世。罗琳正在忙什么呢？她正在写另一本《哈利·波特》。

---

publisher *n.* 出版者；出版商   come true 实现

What Are Some Special Rules for Chinese New Year?

Chinese New Year is a special holiday. It starts on the first new moon of the Chinese *calendar* between January 21 and February 19. The New Year celebration ends fifteen days later on the day of the full moon. Chinese New Year is a very old *celebration*. The Chinese do something different on each day. People believe many old superstitions about this holiday. There

---

中国新年的特殊传统是什么？

新年是中国一个非常特别的节日，它开始于中国农历的第一轮新月，一般是1月21日到2月19日之间，新年的庆祝活动要持续15天，在月圆那天即正月十五时结束。新年是一个非常古老的节日，每个人都要做些不同的事情。人们相信许多关于这个节日的古老习俗，如何打扫

---

calendar *n.* 日历   celebration *n.* 庆祝

are special rules about how people clean and what people look like. There are also rules about how people act.

The Chinese believe that it is very important to have a clean house on New Year's Day. They clean the house before New Year's Day. Then they put away everything they use to clean. The Chinese don't sweep the floor on New Year's Day. They think they will sweep away good luck. After New Year's Day, they sweep again. First they sweep the *dirt* from the door to the middle of the room. Then they sweep the dirt from the middle of the room to the *corners* of the room. They leave the dirt there for five days. On the fifth day, they sweep the dirt to the back door. The Chinese believe that it is bad luck to sweep the dirt to the front door.

The way people look on New Year's Day is also important. The Chinese do not wash their hair on New Year's Day. They believe they will wash away good luck. People also like to wear red clothes on

---

卫生，人们如何穿戴都有特殊要求，人们如何做事也有一定说法。

中国人认为新年打扫房屋非常重要，新年到来之前将房屋打扫干净，然后把打扫工具都收起来。新年那天是不能扫地的，因为他们认为这样会把好运扫走。新年那天过后，他们又开始打扫卫生。首先，将灰尘从门口扫到房屋中间，然后再把灰尘从房屋中间扫到角落里，并在那里放五天，在第五天把尘土扫到后门，将尘土扫到前门会被认为很不吉利。

新年那天，穿戴也非常重要。人们在这一天不能洗头，否则会把好运洗走。人们喜欢在新年那天穿红色衣服，红色是一种鲜艳、愉快的颜色，会给将来带来好运。

---

dirt *n.* 灰尘；尘土

corner *n.* 角落

New Year's Day. Red is a bright, happy color. It will bring good luck for the future.

The Chinese also have superstitions about how people act on New Year's Day. Older people give children and unmarried friends little red *envelopes* with money inside. The money is for good luck. People do not say bad or unlucky words. They do not say the word four because it sounds like the word for death. The Chinese never talk about death on New Year's Day. They also do not talk about the past year. They talk about the new year and new beginnings.

Today, some Chinese believe in these rules and some do not. But many people practice the rules. They are special *traditions*. The rules are part of Chinese culture and history.

在新年那天还有很多其他习俗。老人会给孩子和没结婚的朋友红包，钱象征着好运。人们不能说不好听或不吉利的话，比如"4"，因为它是"死"的谐音。人们也从来不会谈及死亡及和去年有关的话题，所有的话题都是新年和新的开始。

今天，有些中国人仍对此深信不疑，有些则不。但许多人都按这些习俗去做，因为这都是特殊的传统，是中国文化和历史的一部分。

---

envelope *n.* 信封　　　　　　　　　　　　tradition *n.* 惯例；传统

31

Where Is Buckingham Palace?

Buckingham Palace is in London, England. *Buckingham Palace* was built around 1705. It is famous because Queen Elizabeth of England lives there. She became queen in 1952.

Buckingham Palace is a big and beautiful building. A flag flies at the palace. It flies on top of the palace when the queen is there. Queen Elizabeth and her family live

---

白金汉宫在哪里?

白金汉宫坐落在英国伦敦，大约是在1705年建成的，由于英国女王伊丽莎白曾在此居住，因此闻名海内外，伊丽莎白于1952年成为女王。

白金汉宫是一幢既宏伟又漂亮的建筑，宫殿上有一面国旗。女王在时，旗帜升到顶端，伊丽莎白女王和她的家人住在第二层，办公地点也在

Buckingham Palace 白金汉宫（英国皇宫）

on the second floor of the palace. The queen also has her office at the palace. Presidents, kings, and *politicians* meet with her. Queen Elizabeth often asks important people to eat dinner at the palace. She also has three garden parties in the summer. She invites 9,000 people to each party! A lot of people meet the queen.

Buckingham Palace is like a small town. It has a police station, a hospital, two post offices, a movie theater, a swimming pool, two sports clubs, a garden, and a lake. The palace has about 600 rooms. About 400 people work there. Two people have very unusual jobs. They take care of the clocks. There are 300 clocks in Buckingham Palace!

Queen Elizabeth's day starts at 7:00 in the morning. Seven people take care of her. One person *prepares* her bath, and another person prepares her clothes. Another person takes care of her dogs. The queen loves dogs. Right now, she has eight dogs. Every day, a man brings food for the dogs to Queen Elizabeth's room. The queen

---

宫殿里，在那里会见总统、国王和政客们。女王还经常邀请一些重要人物到宫殿聚餐，夏天她要举办三次花园宴会，每次都有九千多人来参加，许多人都见过女王。

白金汉宫像个小镇，里面有警察局、医院、两个邮局、一个电影院、一个游泳池、两个体育俱乐部、一个花园和一个湖泊。整个宫殿共有六百个房间，大约四百人在这里工作。其中有两个人的工作很特别，他们需要照看宫殿里三百多个时钟。

伊丽莎白女王的一天从早上7:00开始。有七个人照顾她的饮食起居。有的为她沐浴作准备，有的为她准备衣服，还有人专门照看她的狗。女王非常喜欢狗，如今她共养了八条狗。每天，有专人把狗食送到她房间，女王用银勺把狗食放在碗里。

---

politician *n.* 政治家；政客

prepare *v.* 准备

puts the food in the bowls with a silver spoon.

At 8:30 every morning, the queen has breakfast with her husband, Prince Philip. They drink a special coffee with hot milk. During breakfast, a *musician* plays Scottish music outside. Then Queen Elizabeth works in her office the rest of the morning. After lunch, she visits hospitals, schools, or new buildings.

It is very interesting to eat dinner at Buckingham Palace. You have to follow rules. Queen Elizabeth starts to eat first, and then everybody eats. When the queen finishes eating, everybody finishes eating. You can't leave the table during dinner. The queen never accepts a telephone call during dinner, even in an *emergency*.

People visit the rooms in Buckingham Palace in August and September. There are wonderful things to see, like paintings and *statues*. Don't forget that Queen Elizabeth is one of the richest people in the world.

每天早晨8:30，女王和她的丈夫菲利浦亲王共进早餐，他们喝那种加有热牛奶的特别咖啡。用餐的时候，有音乐家在一旁演奏苏格兰音乐，接下来，上午的时间女王在办公室办公。午餐过后，她会去参观医院、学校或一些新建筑。

在白金汉宫进餐是件非常有趣的事情。在这里，你必须遵守规矩，只有在女王开始用餐后，其他人才能开始。当女王用完餐后所有的人也都得结束进餐，在这期间，你不能离开餐桌。女王在用餐期间不会接任何电话，即使是最紧急的情况。

每年的八月和九月是白金汉宫对外开放的时间。宫里有许多奇妙的东西，如名画、雕塑等供人们观赏。别忘了，伊丽莎白女王是世界上最富有的人之一。

---

musician *n.* 音乐家   emergency *n.* 紧急情况

statue *n.* 雕像；塑像

32

Why Are Cows Special in India?

About one billion people live in India. Many people live on small farms. They live a quiet and *simple* life. The family takes care of the farm and the animals. The most important animal on the farm is the cow. The cow helps on the farm in two ways. It gives milk to the family, and it works on the farm.

为何印度的奶牛很特别？

印度大约有十亿人口，很多人住在小农场里，过着安静、简单的生活。他们的工作是照看农场和牲畜。最重要的牲畜是奶牛。奶牛对农民来说有两种作用：产奶和在农场耕作。

---

simple *adj.* 简单的

The farmers do not make a lot of money. They can't buy machines to help them do their work. Also, the weather is a problem in India. In June, July, August, and September, there's a lot of rain. The ground gets very wet. Then the ground gets soft. A machine cannot work on soft ground, but a cow can work. Cows also do not cost a lot of money. They don't need *gasoline* or repairs like machines.

Farmers care about their cows very much. They want their cows to be happy. The farms aren't busy at certain times of the year. At these times, people wash and *decorate* their cows. Americans like to wash their cars, and Indians like to wash their cows! Two times a year, there are special celebrations for the cows. These celebrations are like Thanksgiving in the United States.

Old cows cannot work on farms. In India, it is against the law to

---

由于农民收入不高，他们没有能力购买农用机械。另外，印度的天气也是个大问题，一般，六、七、八、九月的降水量很大，地面很潮湿，随后变得很松软，而机器不能在松软的土地上耕作，但奶牛可以。它们不仅成本低，而且不需要汽油或维修。

农民非常爱护奶牛，都希望它们能开心。农场没活的时候，农民便会清洗和打扮奶牛。就像美国人喜欢洗车一样，印度人喜欢给奶牛打扫卫生。一年中人们会专门为奶牛举行两次特殊的庆祝活动，就像美国人庆祝感恩节一样。

奶牛一旦变老就不能在农场上耕作，但印度法律不允许人们随意屠

---

gasoline *n.* 汽油　　　　　decorate *v.* 装饰

kill a cow. So farmers send their old cows away from the farm. The cows walk around free in the streets. Sometimes men sell grass in the street. People buy the grass and give it to the cows. People also give their own food to the cows, and cars are careful not to hit the cows. There are special animal hospitals for old or sick cows. The *government* and some rich people *pay for* these hospitals.

People in other countries do not understand why the Indian government spends money on cows. There are many poor people in India who need money. Indians say that Americans spend more money on cats and dogs. People in India *care for* over 200 million cows every year. They have cared for cows for a long time. It is a tradition that is thousands of years old.

杀奶牛，于是人们就把奶牛赶出农场，这些被赶出去的奶牛就在大街上闲逛。有时会有人在大街上卖青草，人们会买些青草来喂这些闲逛的奶牛。人们还把自己的食物分给奶牛吃，开车时人们也特别小心以免撞着奶牛。印度还有一些专门为照顾老的或生病的奶牛开设的动物医院，这些医院靠政府和有钱人资助。

其他国家的人很不理解印度政府为何在奶牛身上花费这么大，毕竟在印度还有许多贫苦人民等待援助。印度人解释说就像美国人花费许多钱在猫狗身上一样，他们每年都会照顾二十亿头奶牛，这习惯已经保持了几千年，成为传统了。

---

government *n.* 政府

pay for 为……而付钱

care for 照顾；关心

33

How Do Mexicans Celebrate the Day of the Dead?

At the end of October, Mexicans prepare to celebrate the Day of the Dead. The Day of the Dead celebration is two days: November 1 and November 2. On these days, Mexicans remember their dead friends and *relatives*. Relatives are people in your family.

People are not sad on the Day of

墨西哥人是如何庆祝死亡日的？

每年十月底，墨西哥人便开始着手准备庆祝死亡日。死亡日的庆祝有两天：十一月一号和二号。这两天，墨西哥人缅怀他们死去的朋友和家族中死去的亲人。

死亡日到来时人们并不悲伤，相反他们却很高兴。在死亡日的前几

relative *n.* 亲戚

the Dead. They are happy. Markets and shops sell special things before the Day of the Dead. They sell *candles*, flowers, candies, and chocolates that look like *skulls* or bones. They also sell bread called Bread of the Dead. The bread looks like skulls or bones, too!

Families believe that their dead relatives and friends are going to visit them. They make an *altar* in their home for their dead visitors. An altar is a special table with pictures of the dead person. People put flowers, candles, and some of the dead person's favorite things on the altar. The family also puts the dead person's favorite food and drinks there. People leave many different kinds of food and drinks: coffee, water, rice and beans, chicken, fruit, and the special bread and candies for the Day of the Dead. The family also leaves a bowl with water and a clean *towel*. This is for the dead visitors to wash their hands before the meal. Then the family lights the candles and

天，市场和商店都出售一些很特别的东西，例如蜡烛，鲜花，糖果，和像骷髅或骨头似的巧克力。他们还出售像骷髅和骨头似的面包，并把它称为死亡面包。

人们都认为他们死去的亲戚朋友会回来拜访他们，于是都在家里为他们设了祭坛。祭坛上放些鲜花，蜡烛和一些死去亲人们最喜欢的东西。他们还把死者最喜欢的食物和饮料放在那。为迎接死亡日，人们都会准备不同种类的食物和饮料：咖啡，水，米饭，大豆，鸡肉，水果和特别的面包及糖果。人们还会放碗水和一条干净的毛巾以便让回来拜访的死者在吃饭前洗手，然后一家人便点燃蜡烛等着死者的拜访。

candle *n.* 蜡烛
altar *n.* 祭坛

skull *n.* 颅骨；头骨
towel *n.* 毛巾

waits for the dead person to visit them.

At midnight, the family leaves the house. They go to the *graves* of their relatives. A grave is the place in the ground where people put a dead body. The family cleans the grave. They also decorate it with flowers and candles. Then they have a picnic on the grave with special food and drinks. They tell stories about the dead person and talk to the dead person. They eat, drink, play music, and sing.

Different parts of Mexico have different Day of the Dead traditions. Today, in many big towns, Mexican families get together to have a special dinner at home. They eat the Bread of the Dead at this meal. The Bread of the Dead has a toy *skeleton* in it. The Mexicans believe that the person who gets the toy skeleton will have good luck.

午夜时分，一家人便赶去亲戚的墓地。墓地是用来埋葬尸体的地方。他们不仅把墓地打扫得干干净净，还用鲜花，蜡烛把墓地装饰起来。然后在墓地上野餐，享用他们带来的特别食品和饮料，他们谈论死者的种种往事，并和死者聊天。大家一边吃、喝，一边演奏音乐或唱歌。

在墨西哥，不同的地方用不同的方式庆祝死亡日。现在，在许多城镇上，一到死亡日，一家人便团聚在一起吃顿特别的晚餐。聚餐时人们要吃死亡面包，死亡面包里有个玩具骨架，墨西哥人认为吃到有玩具骨架的人会交好运。

---

grave *n.* 墓穴；坟墓

skeleton *n.* 骨架

Who Are the Inuit?

The *Inuit* are special people. The old name for Inuit was "Eskimo". Eskimo means "eater of meat". In 1977, the Eskimos changed their name to "Inuit". Inuit means "the people" in their language. They live in very cold places: *Siberia*, Alaska, Canada, and Greenland. These are the coldest parts of the world.

There are about 120,000 Inuit in the world

谁是因纽特人？

因纽特是个非常特殊的民族，原先把他们称作爱斯基摩人，爱斯基摩的意思是"食肉者"。1977年，爱斯基摩改名为因纽特。因纽特是"人民"的意思。他们居住在世界最寒冷的地方：西伯利亚、阿拉斯加、加拿大和格陵兰岛。

今天世界上共有十二万因纽特人，加拿大就有两万。他们中有的人在离北极非常近的地方定居，因纽特人是最早在加拿大生活的人类。

Inuit *n.* 因纽特人

Siberia *n.* 西伯利亚

today. Canada has 20,000 Inuit. Some live very close to *the North Pole*. The Inuit were the first people of Canada.

In the past, the Inuit *hunted* for all their food. The men traveled in the snow on sleds. About ten dogs pulled a *sled*. The men killed fish and other animals. Then they went home and shared their food with other families. The Inuit used every part of the animal for food and clothes. They usually ate the fish raw. The women made clothes from animal skins. They made shoes from the skins, too. The Inuit had an old custom. The women *chewed* their husbands' shoes at night. Then the shoes were soft in the morning.

The Inuit's life was hard. They lived in houses made of snow. They moved from time to time to hunt animals. Sometimes, the Inuit needed money. Other Canadians needed animal skins. The Inuit sold animal skins to these Canadians. The Inuit and the Canadians

---

过去，因纽特人靠狩猎为生，他们用十只狗拉的雪橇作为行走工具来捕杀鱼和其他动物，然后把猎物带回家和大家一同分享。他们把动物身上的每个部分都做成食物或衣服，还经常生吃鱼。妇女们把动物皮革做成衣服和鞋。因纽特人有个非常古老的传统，妇女们晚上咬丈夫的鞋，这样第二天鞋就变得很松软。

因纽特人的生活非常艰苦，他们住在用雪做的房子里，还要为捕杀动物而不断地搬迁。有时，因纽特人需要钱，而其他加拿大人需要动物皮革，于是他们进行交换，就这样互相帮助。

---

the North Pole 北极
sled *n.* 雪橇

hunt *v.* 狩猎
chew *v.* 咬

helped *each other*.

Today in Canada, the Inuit's lives are very different. Most Inuit live in villages. The villages have from 300 to 1,500 people. The houses are made of wood. The Inuit don't travel in sleds. They ride *snowmobiles*. They buy food and clothes from stores.

The Inuit keep in touch with the rest of the world. They use the telephone, television, and the Internet. They go on *airplanes* to cities in the south of Canada. Inuit boys and girls go to school and have Inuit teachers. They learn about the world. At the same time, the Inuit want to remember their language and traditions. They want to teach their language and traditions to their children.

In the 1970s, the Inuit in Canada wanted to control their land. In 1999, the Canadian government agreed. The government gave the Inuit *a piece of* land in the north of Canada. The name of the Inuit's new land is Nunavut. It means "our land" in their language.

现在因纽特人的生活发生了很大变化。大多数因纽特人住在村庄里，每个村庄大约有三百到一千五百人。他们住在木头房子里。而且不再使用雪橇，取而代之的是雪地机动车。他们还从商店中买取食物和衣服。

因纽特人与外界保持着很密切的联系，他们使用电话，电视机和因特网，还坐飞机去加拿大南部城市旅游。因纽特孩子都去上学，还有专门的因纽特老师教他们认识和了解世界。同时，因纽特人想保留他们的语言和传统，并把这些都传授给他们的孩子。

20世纪70年代，加拿大的因纽特人想控制自己的领土，后来加拿大政府于1999年同意并把加拿大北部的一块土地分给了他们。他们把这块新土地叫"Nunavut"，在他们语言里是"我们的土地"的意思。

---

each other 彼此；互相
airplane *n.* 飞机

snowmobile *n.* 雪地机动车
a piece of 一片；一块

What Is Beatlemania?

Beatlemania is a very strong feeling for the group, the Beatles. The Beatles were four young musicians from Liverpool, England. Their names were John Lennon, Paul McCartney, George Harrison, and Ringo Starr. These four men never took music lessons. They taught themselves to play music.

什么是披头士热？

披头士热是对"披头士"这个组合的一种强烈情结。披头士是来自英国利物浦的四个音乐家:约翰·列侬，保罗·麦卡特尼，乔治·哈里森，林格·斯塔。这四人从来都没上过音乐课，全靠自学成材。

Beatlemania *n.* 披头士狂热

In 1957, John started a group called the Quarrymen. He was sixteen years old. Then he met Paul. They began to write songs and sing together. Soon, George joined them. The group started to play in England and make money. They went to Germany and played *concerts* there, too. The group had different names. They also had some different musicians. In 1962, Ringo joined them. Then John, Paul, George, and Ringo were the Beatles.

The Beatles made their first hit song in 1962. The song was "Love Me Do." In 1963, their song "Please Please Me" was a bigger hit. In all, they had twenty-nine hit songs. By 1963, the Beatles were very popular in England, and Beatlemania started. They had many *fans*. Their fans *screamed* and cried. At concerts, their fans screamed very, very loudly. The Beatles could not hear themselves sing!

1957年，约翰发起了一个叫"采石人"的组合，当时他只有16岁。后来他与保罗相识并开始合作写歌和唱歌，很快乔治也加入了他们。这个组合开始在英国演出并赚钱，还去德国开演唱会。这个组合的名字变换过几次，乐队成员也不固定。直至1962年林格的加入，他们四人组成了"披头士"乐队。

1962年，他们的首支单曲"Love Me Do"在当时引起了极大轰动。1963年，他们创作的"Please Please Me"获得了更强烈的反响。那年，他们共创作了29首歌，都深受欢迎。到1963年，披头士已风靡英国，于是便流行起了披头士热。他们拥有很多歌迷，这些歌迷为他们呐喊哭泣。在演唱会上，歌迷们的忘情呼喊使他们连自己的声音都听不见。

concert *n.* 音乐会
scream *v.* 尖叫

fan *n.* 迷；爱好者

The next year, the Beatles went to the United States. The Americans loved them, and Beatlemania started in America, too. People everywhere copied their clothes and their hair. The Beatles were the most popular rock-and-roll group in the world.

The Beatles *broke up* in 1970. They wanted to play new music. All of the Beatles did interesting, new things. John wrote music with his wife, Yoko Ono. Paul started a new group called "Wings" with his wife, Linda. George and Ringo made their own *records* and gave concerts. Sadly, John was shot dead in New York in 1980. He was forty years old. George became sick and died in 2001.

We still hear Beatles songs on the radio today. Their music and songs will never die.

第二年，"披头士"乐队去美国发展，他们在美国也同样受到极大欢迎，于是披头士热又在美国流行起来了。世界各地的人们开始模仿他们的服饰和发型，他们成为世界上最受欢迎的摇滚乐队。

1970年，由于他们都想尝试新的音乐，乐队解散了。他们四人开始做一些有趣而又新鲜的事：约翰和他妻子一起创作音乐；保罗和他妻子琳达成立了"翅膀"组合；乔治和林格各自发行唱片，开演唱会。不幸的是约翰1980年在纽约被人枪杀了，年仅40岁。2001年，乔治因病去世。

直至今天，收音机里仍播放着披头士的歌曲，我们会永远记住他们的音乐。

---

break up 解散   record *n.* 唱片

36

Where Is the Great Wall?

The Great Wall is in China. The Chinese built the Great Wall thousands of years ago. They wanted to *protect* their country from unfriendly people. First, they built small walls around their towns. Then the *emperor*, Shi Huangdi, joined the walls and built new parts. He wanted to make one long wall—the Great Wall.

万里长城在哪里?

万里长城位于中国境内。几千年前,中国人修建了万里长城以防止外敌入侵。最开始他们将城镇用小城墙围起来,后来,秦始皇将这些围墙连起来,又修建了新的部分。他想建造一堵很长的城墙——长城。

protect *v.* 保护　　　　　　　　　　　　　　　　emperor *n.* 皇帝;君主

Shi Huangdi was the first Qin emperor. The name Qin sounds like Chin. The word China comes from the name Qin. Shi Huangdi made many changes in China. He wanted China to be strong and *modern*. But many Chinese did not like Shi Huangdi. He didn't care about the people. Many people died because of his changes. Thousands of men worked on the Great Wall. It was very hard work. Many men got sick and died. Over one million people died to make the wall. Their bodies are *buried* in the wall. Some people say the Great Wall is "the Wall of Death".

Other Chinese emperors *added* to the wall and made it better. The Ming emperors added thousands of tall, strong buildings in the years 1368-1644. Men stayed in the buildings to protect and repair the wall. They were called guards. Sometimes more than a million guards worked on the wall. They were born on the wall and *grew up*

秦始皇是秦朝的第一位皇帝，"秦"字听起来和"chin"相似，中国(China)这个单词就是来自"秦"字。秦始皇进行了许多改革。他希望中国强大、现代。但是很多人都不喜欢秦始皇，因为他不关心人民，许多人都死在他的一系列变革中。成千上万的人被抓去修长城，这是一件很苦的差事，许多人为此病倒或累死。大约有一百万人丧命于长城的修建工程中。他们的尸体被埋在了长城底下，正如有人所说：万里长城是"死亡之墙"。

以后历代皇帝也陆续加修了长城使它变得更坚固。公元1368到公元1644，明朝皇帝又在长城上增修了几千个高而坚固的烽火台。留在烽火台保护和维修长城的人被称作守卫。有时，有一百多万名守卫在长城上工作，他们生在长城，长在长城，在那结婚生子直至死去。许多守卫一辈子

---

modern *adj.* 现代的

add *v.* 增加

bury *v.* 埋葬

grow up 长大

there. They married there and died there. Many guards lived on the Great Wall all their lives. Sometimes unfriendly men came to the wall to start problems. The guards made a fire to show they needed help. Guards from other parts of the wall ran along the top of the wall to help them.

We don't know *exactly* how long the Great Wall is. There are many different parts of the wall, and some parts fell down. The wall is about 4,000 miles (6,400 kilometers) long and about 25 feet (7.6 meters) high. It is about 15 feet (4.6 meters) wide at the top. Buses and cars can drive along it. Today, the Great Wall is the largest *structure* in the world. Some people say you can see the Great Wall from space. But in 1969, an astronaut who traveled in space said he did not see any buildings—not even the Great Wall.

都生活在长城上。有时，一些不速之客来到长城挑事端，这些守卫们就点火求救，长城上其他地方的守卫就迅速赶来帮助他们。

我们无法准确得知长城究竟有多长。它由不同部分组成，有的地方已经倒塌。长城大约4000英里（约6400公里）长，25英尺（7.6米）高，顶部15英尺（4.6米）宽，公共汽车和小轿车都能通过。长城是当今世上最大的建筑物。有人说在太空都能看见长城。但在1969年，有位宇航员从太空回来却说在太空根本看不见地球的任何建筑，包括长城。

---

exactly *adv.* 正确地；精确地　　　　　　　　　　　　structure *n.* 建筑物